NOBODY'S BABY

Yvonne Gurley

Copyright © 2020 Yvonne Gurley

All rights reserved.

No part of this book may be reproduced or transmitted in any form or by any means, electronic or mechanical, including photocopying, recording, or otherwise, without the prior written permission of the author.

This book is a memoir. It is the author's true story. However, over the years multiple women have shared their story with her, and she decided to intertwine the other women's experiences, thoughts, and expressions with hers to create the main character. Names and characteristics have been changed, events have been compressed, and dialogue has been recreated.

www.thoughtsofthetouched.wordpress.com

First Edition

ISBN:

978-1-7344351-0-8, 978-1-7344351-1-5, 978-1-7344351-2-2

Acknowledgments

Teachers:

Mrs. Belynda Ford and Mrs. Carolyn Owens - Thank you for discovering my talent. Most people are not sure of their purpose until much later in life. However, you two amazing women gave me the blessing of knowing I was a writer at the age of twelve. I could have been just another student passing through but you didn't let me complete the sixth grade without knowing exactly what I was destined to do.

Ms. Bullock - Thank you for always making this shy girl read out loud to the class and seeing so much potential in me opening my mouth to talk.

Mrs. Bonnie Dove - Thank you for being not just my teacher but my friend. You drilled in me I was special. You told me it was okay to be different. You made High School so much easier for me. You encouraged me to laugh out loud as you would always laugh whenever you heard me laughing. My joy was truly your joy too.

Mrs. Jennifer Paul - Thank you for always being so positive. You showed me the freedom in journalism. I put so much thought into taking pictures even if it's just with my phone. I look at nature through a different lens. When I see people, I truly try to "see people." You forever changed me as a writer.

Mrs. Renee Austin-Banks - Thank you for taking me to lectures after class and telling me I wasn't just a writer. I couldn't see it at the time or understand why you wanted to push me past just writing. You saw something I couldn't see. You continued to encourage me even long after I left your class. I wish there were more teachers like you.

Loved Ones:

My daughter Essence - There is so much I could say, I could write another book to acknowledge all you do. Your spirit, your love, and your compassion are more than inspiring. You have made me better in every way possible. You have been the gift that keeps on giving the older and older you get. You came into this world knowing exactly how to love me and I'm forever grateful to be your mom.

My big sisters, Bridgette and Tracee - Thank you for being mothers when I needed you to be. Thank you for all the hugs and forehead kisses. Thank for crying when I cried and laughing when I laughed. Thank you for supporting my journey and sharing your journey with me.

My husband, Pashad Holloway - Thank you for staying on me, for pushing me to finish what I start. Thank you for believing in me more than myself at times. Thank you for truly seeing me, the real me. Thank you for your persistence and your patience. Thank you for maturing me in the ways I swore I was already mature. Thank you for attempting to make me laugh every single day. Thank you for loving me.

Special People:

Natasha Adams - I miss you every day. You were already my angel before you left. Thank you for all the food you cooked just for me, all the movies we watched, the songs we sang, all the yard sales and all the grocery store runs. The time we spent meant the world to me. Thank you for hearing my heart and sharing yours with me.

Robin Means - Thank you for always opening your doors. I came over way too much but you never showed me that. Thank you for including me. Thank you for all the Oprah we watched. Thank you for sharing your family with me.

Quintyn Seals - Thank you for always coming to my rescue even when you were in another state. Thank you for your thoughtfulness. Thank you for all the breaks you gave me from being a single mom. Thank you for putting up with me. Thank you for your kindness and generosity. Thank you for the unconditional love you always gave to me and my daughter.

Mrs. Carolyn B. Nichols - Thank you for seeing yourself in me. Thank you for caring. Thank you for giving me so much love, light, and wisdom. Your existence in my life will always be a gift from God.

Dr. Kim Yada - Thank you for being so much more than my therapist. You are unforgettable and a treasure to my heart. You taught me the truth in sanity and unpacked all the lies I told myself. I'll forever be grateful.

Jane Anderson, Jesse Thacker, and Dana Cook Anderson - A nine to five became so much more when I had the pleasure of working with you. You looked past my job description and saw the person in me. You shared yourselves with me and work was so therapeutic. You came into my life when my dreams of being a writer were far behind me. You woke up my destiny and encouraged me to write again. Thank you for pulling me out of the shell I crawled into and planned to never leave.

Influencers:

Thank you to all the women I had the honor of meeting over the years and sharing your stories with me. Thank you for inviting me into your conscious and sharing your secrets. You reminded me over and over again that you story was my story and inspired me to write our story. May our secrets heal just one more woman or girl and let her know she's not alone.

Thank you to my beta readers. You encouraged me that this story was needed and missing from the world. When I thought it was too heavy you told me it was but it was necessary. Just like all the women whom inspired me with their truths you told me it was your truth as well. You taught me pain has no preference in location, race, language, or financial status.

> God, how could I possibly thank you with words? It seems as though there's no language that could give you the honor you deserve. Thank you for giving me this story and others' stories. Thank you for never giving up on me, for teaching me

your ways. Thank you for sending so many people whom were an extension of your love, grace, and mercy. Thank you for being all that you are and who you are to me. Thanking for having a plan for my life and sharing it with me so that I might have hope to survive.

Prologue

I wanted to let the world know
That you can be born into this world
    "nobody's baby"
Nobody but Gods' anyway
And somebody's maybe

I never realize or feel like nobody loves me
Until somebody says that they do
And I find out it's not true
Then I come to the realization that they don't
I try hard to make them until I realize that they
    won't

Now I'm stuck in the same old hurt again
She's lonely, depressed, without a friend
Not because I really have no friends
But because in my mind no one understands

So, I isolate myself, write a few poems
And cry in the shower until the midnight hour
Oh, whoa it's me, negative Nancy, sad Susie
        Yvonne Gurley

I am hurt again

The pain is so deep this time
My soul feels like it burning
They say we should get to the root of the problem
Find out where it all started
See if we can solve them

Many years of cursing, screams, and fights
Many years spent crying alone and sleepless nights
Many years of thinking this can't be my life
Many years not knowing my thinking was right

We go wrong when we accept
Abuse to be something that's true
Abuse accepted are lies told to you

I made excuses, I ran and I hid Where
was my protection?
I was just a kid
I ran away just trying to escape
Yet every yard I entered
Was another one of hells' gates

The good news is, I finally got free

I finally got away from hell

But not until I realized
The freedom was inside me

So, what did I do, when I finally got free?
I started my journey, my journey to finding me
Many more years would pass before I would see
Why I survived, and the plan God had for me

The only difference between a "smart" person and a person who doesn't seem smart is the "smart" person has figured out how to help themselves.

1   Just Don't

Hello, I'm Stacey. I'm the youngest of four. I have two sisters and a brother. Maybe you know me and maybe you don't or maybe you are me. I'm one of those deep thinkers. I find myself having to dumb my conversation down to things I really don't care or think about in order to have conversations with most people. I'm not saying I'm one of those people who use a bunch of big words that most people don't use when conversing. It's just that my thoughts normally go past the obvious wonders of the world. You see, I'm hardly ever where I really am at any moment. Could be a "writer's thing," I don't know, but I'm usually in my own world. Typically, I am in some sort of deep thought; sadly, it's usually when people are talking to me about one of those things, I mentioned that I don't care or ever think about when I drift into my own contemplations.

"Hey Stacey, my brother Wolf says he likes you."

"Aww girl, whatever!"

Even as far back as sixth grade, I never knew Love, and as far as I was concerned, Love never knew me either.

Yvonne Gurley

We spent a lot of time trying to find each other, though there were some mistaken identities along the way. I was always aware I needed it; Love knew I needed it, too. I just regret all the things I did to find it. All the missteps and faults I made and the people I hurt could have been avoided had I known that all I ever had to do was be still. I tried to pinpoint where Love was but I never could. I couldn't fathom the possibility of Love wanting to find me just as mercilessly as I wanted to find it. Yet Love knew my location all along. The problem was I wouldn't be still!

There's a "Just Don't" compartment I've created in my brain. You see, I'm one to self-sabotage. I think too much, I do too much, and boy, do I often say too much. It comes with being analytical. This compartment is long overdue and very necessary. Mastering self-control has gotten to a whole new level. I'm also a bit of a control freak, however not with other people. My problem takes off when I feel I have no control over me. I want what I want when I want it.

Having this attitude has gotten me into more than words can describe, like being a patient in a mental hospital. If that doesn't float your boat, how about becoming an addict or being in a relationship with an addict. Lastly, I ended up in the kind of trouble that causes one to lose everything, almost my life. Sometimes, it's not that you need to be saved from anyone or anything; sometimes you just need to be saved from yourself.

Had I created this "Just Don't" compartment a long time ago, I'd be so much further in my life. I'd be much less broken and in less need of repair. Currently, like a lot of people, I'm stuck in the "wannabe" category. I'm a wannabe writer, poet, singer/songwriter, actress, and married. That's not even the end of my wannabe list since it could go on forever.

Nobody's Baby

There are so many things, as well as people, that should have a place in my little compartment. The words I've uttered and the things I've done are endless when it comes to "Just Don't." Those earlier examples were not just examples, by the way. I really use to be an addict, but let's not jump straight to crack or heroin. I was the kind of addict that some of your finest everyday citizens become. Also, being in a relationship with an addict really happened too, except this time go right ahead and jump to something like cocaine. What's worse was it was more than just a relationship—seven years, a kid, and a ring kind of relationship. Lastly, the whole in-patient in a mental hospital scenario really happened too. So when I said this compartment was long overdue, I really meant it. What I've just mentioned is not even everything.

I'd say loneliness is one of the biggest reasons this box was implemented. Being, or even just feeling, alone gets me into so much trouble. I've made some horrible decisions mainly because of loneliness or the fear of being alone. It's a dangerous place to be for a lot of people. Loneliness can rob you of your pride and your dignity. It can make you feel so low and undeserving of anything. It tends to make people lower their standards and do all the things they said they'd never do.

Don't judge, though, because while you're doing these things and being this person you don't even recognize, it all seems worth it. The contemplation of being alone for just one more day or just one more moment made me want to scream, or worse.

This thing, this monster, has a cousin known as greed. You see, the cousin is not just satisfied with not being alone. Greed wants to feel and be known, too. So now one isn't just running from loneliness because it becomes more complicated; not only is there a need to be tolerated, but there's also a need to be understood.

For me, the feeling of loneliness and being misunderstood started early. I had a "Just Don't" box then, too, but it had a totally different use. When anybody, especially a child, experiences or is exposed to abuse, it automatically creates a sense of isolation. Kids do not talk to each other about how they're being abused at home or how they are witnessing abuse at home. Having to keep this experience a secret builds that first compartment and fills it with thoughts of "I'm the only one" or "No one would understand." As common as abuse always has
been, it's just as much been a secret. It's the biggest, wellkept secret I know. My "Just Don't" back then contained more "Just don't cry" or "Just don't scream," but the biggest was "Just don't tell anybody." Funny how up until a few years ago my "Just Don't" box was left with

nothing but "Just don't feel."

Oh yeah, see, I got smart—or so I thought. By the time my addiction was in full effect, my only goal in life was to not feel. To me, feeling anything was the route to all pain, be it physical or emotional. For six years I made sure I felt *nothing*. Being numb allowed me to completely do away with having a "Just Don't" box. I became a zombie, a walking shell with no soul and certainly no filter. For years, it didn't matter what anyone said or did to me because I was bulletproof. However, this worked in the other direction as well because I had no regard or consideration for what I said or did to others.

Nobody's Baby

Ever have a gut punch to the soul? I have, and on more than one occasion. Ever thought you were an honest person and found out just how false that was? I did! I would soon find out I was quite far from being an honest person. What was worse was the main person I had been lying to was myself, therefore I couldn't even begin to be honest with others.

You might be wondering how such a thing could happen, but for starters, I didn't even know how I was doing. No, really! I could not answer one of the worse questions a person could ask me. I was doing all that I could so that no one would ask me, "How do you feel?" I stayed busy so I never had to ask myself.

"Are you okay?" Anytime someone asked me this I always thought to myself, "Is this some sort of trick question?" Sometimes I even asked the person if it was simply because I was unsure. Let's be honest, who's ever really okay when being asked, "Are you okay?" My usual reply was, "No worries," unless I branched out like everyone else with a simple, "I'm fine, and you?" If I actually told people exactly how I really felt and how I was really doing, someone, I'm sure, would have had me committed.

I must take a second and laugh to myself, as when I originally wrote these feelings down I hadn't yet been to the mental hospital. I guess I spoke it up or "wrote it up." I guess there really is power in words after all, even if you write them.

There's some honesty for you. How do you like it? I decided I'm going to be completely honest with myself and as honest as possible with others—or so I thought.

All the missteps and faults I made and the people I hurt could have been avoided had I known that all I ever had to do was be still.

2 Realization

Let me start by saying I had more than an issue with being alone, but I had issues with the realization of self-worth as well. In the most southern way, I can say this, if you don't know who you are and what your worth is then you are in trouble. If, by the time you even think you're coming into your own and you don't have your identity and your selfworth in check, you have a problem. Your identity and dignity problems are guaranteed to take you on the ride of your life, which can be anything but fun and amusing. Just imagine riding a rollercoaster for years and new people keep hopping on but you can never get off. Who could even survive that without potentially ending up with some issues?

What about standards, you ask; well, what about them? I'm not sure I had set any real standards for myself, let alone others. My foundation for relationships and friendships was extremely low and dysfunctional. Treating people poorly was my normal from the very beginning. Therefore, I kept people around who treated me pretty crappy because that was how I was raised.

What's worse was whenever I met people who attempted to treat me well, it would actually feel like abuse and I'd cut that person off from my life faster than he or she would see it coming. After that I'd hop back in the cycle of finding more people to treat me crappy again, providing me with what was comfortable and normal to me, though it was far from it. So, as I mentioned before, don't judge. Loneliness is a beast that can cause one to be completely out of character. I can admit to being out of order for a long time.

Are people really crazy or are we just frustrated with sanity? I was a lost soul but I was the kind of lost soul that was fully aware I was lost. That notion alone could drive anyone mad. Think about it: How frustrated do you get when your GPS leads you to a deserted field? It never does it right away, it seems to always lead you on for quite a while, building up your hope of experiencing something new, something different, something other than what you've known and felt your whole life. That's what it's like to be cognizant you're adrift. It's realizing your GPS is leading you nowhere over and over again until finally there's no hope of getting anywhere at all. The problem is turning back around is not an option. I knew too much to turn back but not enough to move ahead. Why couldn't I be the type of person who didn't know, who wasn't so aware? I was mindful of my past and my present yet had no idea what to do about the future.

I originally wrote so much more in this chapter, but it was just much more of a person I thought I was. Looking back, I was just touching on the subject of my worth in life but I hadn't fully grasped it. Back then, I was still hearing the whispers of things I could never do and things I could never have. I was caught up in the land of wishful thinking. I had a lot of hopes and dreams when I first attempted to write this chapter but honestly, I still didn't truly believe they could come true, at least not for me.

Nobody's Baby

There comes a point in everyone's life if they'll allow it, in which God gives you that break and shows you that "Yes, even you" moment.

3 The Beginning of the End

A woman's biggest mistake she can make in her life, I think, would be to make a habit of running to a man, instead of running to God. I was about to learn this lesson the hard way. It took me almost my entire twenties to get this.

To break down the psychology of such behavior, seeking a man was forced upon me at first. With my father being absent and my mother not being an affectionate person as well as absent-minded, the only affection I received was from my abusers. It was the only time I was held or comforted in any way. Though it might seem odd, during the abuse, a person may not realize the comfort he or she finds in it. I despised my abusers yet the discomfort was the only comfort I knew.

Like most eighteen-year-olds, I thought I had it all figured out. You know how it goes, by the end of your senior year you have this big plan for your life and oddly enough you think it's all going to work out. All the possibilities you come up with are almost always positive. Back then, I would have called you crazy if you told me that within the next three years I would be a college dropout, playing stepmother to three kids, suffer layoffs, have my own kid, and become an addict. No one could have told me that for me to actually believe it.

I had just graduated from high school and two months later Byron came along. He couldn't have come at a worse time in my life, though it was perfect timing for him. I thought I was ok, but boy was I wrong. Right before I graduated from high school, I experienced my first lay off and my first break up—I wasn't in a good place. I didn't realize it because I had been having so much fun. I picked up my first rebound to numb the pain of my breakup. Not only that but at the time I also thought I wanted to give a career in law a try. I had worked in insurance and it was all I knew, but I figured why not try law.

I immediately got a job at a law firm working as a legal debt collector; though I felt the odds were against me, I was still proud of myself. I started the job and it seemed all right at first. I was still able to go to school at night so logically, to me, I was still on the right track. By that time I was completely over my breakup and feeling pretty good, I thought. As it turned out, my coworkers loved to party. Most of them were all in their twenties, though some were knocking on thirty; none the less, it made for a dang good time.

Byron was that one random guy that hangs with all the females at work trying to become every woman's best friend. It worked, the parties, and getting advice about men and relationships from Byron; I was not in any pain, or so I thought. With that said, I decided that my boy toy and I were going in different directions so that ended naturally. We just stopped talking with no communication about it. I was enjoying my new life and new freedom. I was so excited about it, I completely forgot about my abusive childhood—though one can never really forget.

Nobody's Baby

I was going to college parties and hanging out with a whole new group of people who, at the time, I considered friends. It was fun, but that fun wouldn't last very long.

In the beginning, it was normal co-worker fun. I had no special relationship with anyone of the opposite sex though I had gotten close to some of the women. I was even considering being roommates with one of them but that dream died very fast.

Speaking of dying, I got the news that one of my childhood friend's mother passed away—I was devastated! That woman meant the world to me. Her house was one of my many escapes during my abusive childhood. I would run to her as often as I could; I never spoke to her about it but I believe deep down a part of her always knew. She was only in her thirties when she passed so no one saw it coming at all.

For me, I was in a dark place. I didn't know how to be there for my friend when I felt like I had lost my mother, too. For the first time in my life, the writer didn't have a word to say. Selfishly, I ran and I hid, not being able to handle her death or support my friend. Though it has been over a decade, I still find myself mourning her.

Unfortunately, my days just kept getting darker. My father had started writing me letters after being absent for twelve years. I assumed his newfound interest had something to do with his schizophrenia and it wouldn't allow him to just call me; none the less, I was pleased with the letters. I decided to return letters with him as a way to stay connected. Yet I remember just like it was yesterday when one of my letters came back to me. I had only been communicating with him for a few months and in a blink of an eye, he was gone again.

There I was mourning not just my friend's mother, but my father as well. He hadn't died but after leaving me once more, he was dead to me for almost thirteen years after those letters stopped. My heart was rippling with pain and it hurt so bad that I couldn't even cry. It was if something just shut down inside of me.

During this dark time, I began to indulge in drinking. I was never very good at getting drunk because I have a weak or sensitive stomach. I couldn't take a shot to save my life without vomiting immediately after. None the less, I still tried to drink as much as I could and as often as I could to numb the pain. I had begun to flunk out of my first semester of college. This wasn't like me. In all my years of school, I had never even been to summer school. I wasn't a genius, but I wasn't used to failing any classes either.

Failing classes wasn't my only problem. My relationship with my female friends were falling apart, too. Just my luck that these same friends held power in my livelihood. Once things went south, they arranged to have me fired from the law firm. My dark place seemed to only be getting darker. At the time, Byron was one of the few people I had.

Byron was part of the party crew of coworkers I'd hang out with. I never had a real interest in him or even looked at him in that way at all. Truth be told, he wasn't my type. I openly admit to being superficial and let's just say Byron didn't meet the qualifications. Still, I thought he was cool to hang out with. Anyway, Byron had learned about the obscurity I faced and offered his condolences. He was seven years older than me so I thought it was safe

Nobody's Baby

to allow him into my world as a friend—an older more mature friend. I was in a world of pain and really needed a friend. Actually, I needed Jesus but I didn't know that.

While in my dark hole, we began to talk more often and he got me flowers to cheer me up. Actually, he offered to help in any way that he could. He showed this friendliness to all of the other female coworkers so I saw no harm and really thought he was a stand-up guy. One day though, on a very terrible night and I do mean very, a line was crossed. Crossing that line was the start of the end for me.

Everyone at the law firm knew of Byron's marital problems; however, no one cared enough to talk about it. On the night in which he crossed the line, I was giving him a ride home. While on the way we pass his wife on her way to see another man. I had been witnessing her affair since my start of college, as she was having this affair with one of the professors. I had no idea this woman was Byron's wife.

Back to that evening in question, he appeared to be so hurt after seeing her. I felt compassion to be there for him. He relayed all the stories of how he did everything he could to be such a good husband and father yet she was just so unappreciative. I'd learn later just how false all his stories were and how his wife had every right to be cheating on him. In my eyes, he was only getting exactly what I felt he deserved at the time.

I was eighteen and didn't fully grasp what I was getting myself into. Byron and his wife divorced and he moved in with me. He had a strong attachment to me at first and would act heartbroken every time I had to go to class or anywhere out of his sight for that matter. I was so intrigued by how much he appeared to love me and want me around that I eventually dropped out of college. Somehow, I confused his actions with thinking his behavior was some form of support.

He should have pushed me and my education but he didn't. I'd find out eventually that it was never me that he wanted around so much, but it was access to my car because didn't have one. If I was home, my car was at home. I didn't have the wisdom to recognize his tactics then. He told so many lies about his transportation. The car he claimed he had was his car from high school that had been sitting in front of his parents' house broken down for years.

Right before Byron had moved in, I actually had my entire apartment packed up and I was heading for Tennessee State to attend college with my cousin. I had my mind set on studying journalism and broadcasting to work for some big television network. Obviously, that didn't happen. I flushed those dreams down the toilet when I allowed Byron to convince me to stay. I remained, but my dream of being a writer would be forgotten until I was almost thirty.

> *A woman's biggest mistake she can make in her life, I think, would be to make a habit of running to a man, instead of running to God.*

4   How Come?

Why didn't I realize the obvious? In hindsight, I ask myself thousands of questions. Regardless of what Byron's wife was doing, what about what Byron was doing? I totally dismissed the fact that a line had been crossed with me.

While he was explaining how hurt he was, we never discussed his own affairs and actions. For months, he and his family carried on about how Byron's wife was horrible. Now, when I think back upon it, it was so unfair to both me and her.

I had been brainwashed. No one cared to mention that regardless of what his ex was doing, Bryon was still legally married and had no business being with me, and for more reasons than just being married. For starters, I had just graduated from high school and I was a working college student. Byron was twenty-five with three kids and a wife. Our paths couldn't be more diverse and we couldn't have been more wrong for one another.

I let my emotions make so many decisions for me, which is one of the worse habits to form because your emotions almost always lie. I allowed my emotions to talk me out of my obedience. The biggest trick your emotions play is telling you you're okay when you're not and vice versa. For me, I thought all these events were driving me to a dark place but they weren't. I even blamed failed relationships, both personal and professional. Over time, I blamed my life and bad choices on everything and everyone, except, the true culprit.

Writing this chapter was such a challenge because all I've been asking myself for so long was how come? The negative voices totally took a toll on me. My mind kept saying, "You're so stupid, Stacey" and "Oh my Gosh, Stacey, everything was so obvious" or "Stacey, it's all your fault." I questioned myself about why I didn't see what was to come but then I recalled how young and impressionable I was at the time. If I had the opportunity to write eighteen-year-old Stacey a letter, it would only say one word, "HEAL." Honestly, I shed so many tears over this chapter because that poor girl had no idea that welcoming Byron into her life would almost be the end of her—and for a while, it was the end.

I was still a child when Byron and I met. Not only that, but I was extremely broken. I was so fragmented; one could never count the pieces of my heart. My childhood had completely broken me and I didn't even realize it. I had broken myself. I was so used to keeping my abuse and pain a secret that I kept it a secret from myself. I didn't even confess my feelings to me. My life became filled with so much stuff there was no time to ever address me. My abuse was completely ignored, and the issues that developed from the abuse were also ignored. By the time I became an adult, I treated myself how everyone else treated me, and I mastered how to completely ignore myself, or so I thought.

Many abusers act completely unaware of their actions. None of my abusers have ever been brought to justice and I run into them every now and then; they actually have the nerve to approach as if we had this great relationship. Oh, the anger it used to fill me with! If molestation was something that was once done to the abuser, how could they forget how they felt? This is something I don't understand. How could one forget that first moment of confusion and shame? How could one forget the first imprint of a scar that would last a lifetime? Are abusers really completely unaware?

The day would soon come when I realized I had become my own abuser! After surviving childhood abuse and then enduring even more abuse from bad relationships, I began to abuse myself. I had always abused myself but I didn't know it at the time. No, I wasn't cutting myself or banging my head against things, that's wasn't me. However, in my mind, I was totally whipping my own butt. Being unhappy was my comfort zone—
sadness and depression were all I knew. I can't say that I liked being there, but it was just what was familiar to me.

When I finally got out and into the world, I had no idea how to be happy. I'd been trying to find "my happy. "I was so clueless back then. I wondered what happy would look like. What did it sound like? And most importantly what did it feel like? I made the common mistake of trying to define my happy based on someone else's happy. This was the biggest mistake I ever could have made. I would eventually learn that behind those shades or glasses there were eyes that might not always allow one to see the true color of those eyes clearly. I learned that everyone else was just as clueless as me, or perhaps even less happy than me. I would one day find that one should not define their "happy" based on someone else because you might find that you're the happier one.

Often, I would say to myself, "Stacey, you should smile because you tried. Even in the midst of what you thought were failures you still won because of the lesson learned. After all, the point of all tests was to learn and show you all that you do not understand!" Those words seem ironic to me now because there was so much I didn't understand. Now that I'm no longer ignoring myself, I would say one thing to that eighteen-year-old girl—HEAL. I wish I could go back and warn her, comfort her, and tell her to brace herself for the storms that were sure to come. Then I would tell her, "After you heal, forgive yourself, and then love yourself." Unfortunately, that poor girl looked to Byron as her knight in shining armor when she should have been looking to God. When I ask and answer all of the whys and how come questions, I weep for her. Stacey, the young Stacey, had no clue as to the damage her relationship with Byron would do. All I can ask now is, "Oh Lord, how come?"

For the longest time, the world has been defining depression as some sort of a disorder. It is made to be something ugly and this thing we should all be ashamed to tell the world we suffer from when all along we should have just defined it as being alive. Even animals get depressed sometimes. I mean, even the flowers frown when enough sunlight isn't around. Life does pass all of us by and every day is not always a good day. Sometimes I wake up and it's sunny and other times its grey. So, sue me if one day there is a storm. Is there shame in needing a blanket when you get cold to keep you warm? No, so why is there shame in needing help when you battle depression?

I needed to know that I was not alone. I needed to be aware that had I come forward I would not be stoned for falling victim to some sad days. Young Stacey was crying on the inside but couldn't tell a soul, but no one would ever know because the world defines depression as some sort of illness in your mind. Depression or severe sadness is not a disorder, it's part of being alive and the key is to push through! Eighteen-year-old Stacey, there are so many things I wish I could have told you. I wish you had me and I'm sorry I ignored you. I'm sorry I ignored myself.

I discovered even when I thought I was right I was still wrong! Let me break it down to you. I called myself out when I recognized when and where I was wrong in my life choices; however, I kept making bad choices even though I wasn't necessarily making the exact same decisions. I found myself continuing to be wrong for years! You can't imagine how frustrating life is when you're trying to do better and you're still wrong! The point I'm getting to is to make sure, or in my case find out, if your idea of right is wrong.

I'll explain what I mean by an example. Let's say you are struggling with eating right. You educate yourself and you decide to go with this new eating plan that you read about. You've now created this whole new lifestyle and eating habits according to your understanding of what you read. Time passes and you think you're doing everything right until you realize you are seeing little to no results, or worse your new plan is having the opposite effect on your good intentions to eat or live right.

Here's where we find the importance of the rights in being wrong. I was right for wanting and then attempting to do better, but wrong in doing better according to my understanding only. Just because we understand or think we understand, doesn't always mean our understanding is correct. It's no wonder I kept repeating old habits in new ways!

Let me tell you another way rights can be wrong. Let's say you did try to ask others who "read" the book about your new life plan. You asked them and they got the same understanding that you did, or worse their understanding could be further from being right than your own understanding. Now you're really screwed!

I was screwed because when I entered into those bad relationships and poor friendships, everyone around me was too. I was a bad friend and everyone in my circle was a bad friend too. I treated myself poorly and unfortunately everyone I knew treated themselves this way as well. I'd learn to check my resources! Undoubtedly you should too, if you haven't. If everyone around you is on the same page as you or further behind in the story, they can never tell you how it ends or how to understand. You need people around you who have already read the book and applied the change correctly [Proverbs 3:5 AMP Lean on, trust in, and be confident in the Lord with all your heart and mind and do not rely on your own understanding.]. I can't tell you how long I leaned on only my understanding and when I did ask others, their understanding was just like mine or worse. How was I ever going to heal?

> I am screaming and yelling
>
> Crying out for a hand
>
> I am beating on the walls
>
> Trying to get you to understand I
>
> am screaming

I wrote that poem years ago in the midst of my pain. When I wrote it, I meant it for everybody but me. However, it wasn't until recently that I realized I was talking to me, or I should have been anyway!

How many of us realize that everything we do and don't do is saying something? It represents something whether it's intentional or not. As adults, we don't realize how childish we are. Of course, there are those who try to point it out but who listens to those people, right? All we are trying to do is be heard and understood and when we're not, the world better watch out!

World, young Stacey had been screaming her entire life, begging for somebody, anybody, to please know she was in pain. The only problem was knowing wasn't good enough. She wanted someone to pay and to heal her brokenness. She didn't realize one of the most dangerous things she could do was leave her healing up to someone else. It was dangerous because it would never happen!

Hindsight, the only person I needed to be screaming at was myself! I'm the one who needed to know and understand how much pain I was in. I needed for *me* to care about *me*. I needed me to fix me. Why I thought if I could just get one person to agree with my pain I'd be healed. That was WRONG! With Byron and my friends, my twenties were chockful of a bunch of broken people like me. Guess what a group of broken people do—scream at each other! At that point, you find yourselves competing for whose pain is greater while no one is healing.

I thought that always expressing my hurt I was acknowledging and recognizing my pain, but that was not true. In fact, I was doing what everyone else had done—leaving my hurt up to someone else. I needed to save myself. After all, I'm the one who feels it.

So today I did some screaming and yelling but this time I yelled at myself. All those years telling others about my problems allowed me to not deal with my problems. Every time I came across another person who I thought could surely heal me, he or she failed me every time. Unfortunately, I used this as an excuse to remain broken.

I challenged myself to finally take responsibility and own my brokenness. I wrote a book about my pain that I refused to read. However, I left it on the shelf for the world to read! How can I spend my entire life knowing there's a book somewhere about me that I expect everyone else to read but me? It makes no sense. Don't allow the world to get to know you better than you know yourself! Healing, joy, peace, and happiness can only be found in you and is between God and you. First, you have to know who you are!

I allowed my emotions to talk me out of my obedience.

5 Who Are You?

I burned myself to save the fire. Sounds absurd, doesn't it? It's exactly what I was doing when I stayed with Byron for all those years. I walked right into this relationship which I had no idea had the power to consume me. Can you blame me? After all, Hell's temperature was all I knew.

If you've ever felt this way you're not alone. Byron came in seemingly fully equipped with everything I ever wanted, well almost everything. Although I was never attracted to him physically, I was able to overlook it for a while. He put forth such a great effort at first. His family even joined in on the show. He seemed to be what most would want, dismissing the fact he lacked charm and good looks. Byron appeared to be a true God-fearing, family man. At that point in my life, I had no clue what it looked like for a person to really know God on any level. I couldn't have been more ignorant. He went to church on an occasion and mentioned the Lord every now and then so that was all the proof I needed because that was more than what I was doing.

Yvonne Gurley

I later found out that Byron's ex-wife, Shanelle, also attended as well as worked at the information desk at the same college as one of my sisters. My sister and her friends would talk about Shanelle often, but we never realized who she actually was for so many reasons. One reason was that she was being referred to as "sign language girl." This was her area of study and, along with her awkward social skills, was the reason for the nickname. I mentioned that I witnessed seeing her with the professor; however, I would only ever see her in the car, never up close. Shanelle mentioned her troubled past relationship with Byron at work but he had convinced my sister and I that it was all lies. Everything she stated would eventually be proven to be completely accurate. Unfortunately, because he swayed my family to believe Shanelle was a huge liar looking for pity, we completely dismissed what she had mentioned about Byron. I wished every day that we had listened to her. The longer I stayed with Byron the more I would ask myself who I was. For years, I didn't know who I was and it became evident that I didn't know who he was either. He was exactly like Shanelle said he was and he did all the things she said he would do, and probably more.

Did you know that you could be in love with someone or someone could be in love with you solely based on the situation? I call it "circumstantial love." You have to be careful with this kind of love if one can even call it love at all. This love will have you stuck in a marriage or longterm relationship for years until you find yourself waking up to a miserable nightmare you refer to as your life.

If I have never stated this before, I'm sharing it now. Everything I reiterate is based on my own life experiences, mistakes, and lessons I've learned. Though I read, the things that I share do not come from any book. This book contains all the mistakes I've made and kept making on my journey. I wanted to clarify these truths for one simple

Nobody's Baby

reason—circumstantial love was the biggest driving force in all the mistakes I've made in my life thus far.

The reason why I kept indulging in this kind of love is mainly that I didn't know me and most importantly, I didn't love me. See, when you're leaving your happiness or healing up to other people, you're bound to end up in circumstantial love. There are other reasons this can happen such as financial binds, loneliness, or you're a hurt person altogether. All the same, you may find yourself like I found myself, loving people because my circumstances at the time depended on it, or so I thought.

However, this can also go the other way. Sometimes people will claim to love you only because of their situation and what you can do for them as well. It's still all the same because if you're codependent, you'll end up loving that person because of what you think you're doing for him or her and you like the love you think you're receiving in return. It's a sad truth, people!

Yvonne Gurley

Until recently, I spent my entire adulthood chasing what I felt I lacked as a child. Unfortunately, that was love. I attached myself to anything and anyone whom I thought showed me any kind of love. Doing that was very dangerous because it caused more problems. I created so many circumstances in my life by bringing people into my life who could only give me circumstantial love. This socalled love is and always will be temporary. One can try to drag it out as I did, but it's extremely painful to do and holds you back from so much that is good in life.

When you find out who you are, then you can find out all the "whys" in your character. When I say "why" I mean the explanations for why you are the way you are and why you make poor decisions. I could never get to this conclusion because I made sure I was never alone. Life forced me to be alone and in this, I was forced to learn or die. Chasing my circumstantial love was killing me on the inside each time it came to an end. I got so frustrated that I had to check myself on all levels.

I would say the biggest lesson I learned was you don't have to be in love to know or feel real love. Like a lot of people, I made the mistake of thinking this was the only way to experience love. I created so many circumstances that would allow me to feel what I thought was love. The "love" was always as temporary as my situations though.

It's true, nothing lasts forever. So before you call something love, check yourself. Look at where you are and what's going on in your life and ask yourself if you would love this person if you weren't where you were.

Also, check your emotions. Do you love this person because he or she makes you feel better but only about what's going on at that moment? Find out what you actually do for the other person and make sure their love for you is not circumstantial either. Asking myself these questions helped me weed out false love. It also kept me from finding new ways to repeat old habits.

Chasing my circumstantial love was killing me on the inside each time it came to an end.

"Love must be sincere. Hate what is evil; cling to what is good."
Romans 12:9

6 On the Floor

Text message: "Sis, come get me!" "Come get you, why? Where you at?" "I'm at home, in the bathroom, on the floor." "Why are you on the floor? What's wrong?" "I'll let you know when I find out, just come get me!"

Yvonne Gurley

That was me trying to get my sister to help me. You see, my hallucinations had gotten so bad that I didn't even trust myself or my own thinking, let alone anyone else's. My addiction to pills made it so I could no longer tell if I was coming or going anymore. I had become immune to everything.

At that point, there was no one keeping track of how many pills or what dosages were taken except me. In the days leading up to this conversation with my sister, I had been overdosing pretty much every day. However, everything was different in the days to come.

I suffered from insomnia because of my PTSD. Usually, or eventually, I'd finally crash and get some sleep but not this time. I had been up for days. I was mixing my day pills with my night pills, desperate for a combination that would allow me to finally get some sleep.

If you ever find yourself on the floor, you're onto something. Having spent many years crying my eyes out, I can't tell you how many showers were dedicated to tears. Countless nights of soaking pillows, bathroom stalls I locked myself into, or randomly parking the car to shed a tear, yet after all of that crying, I still found myself back at the same point. No matter where or how pain was shed, it wasn't until I found myself on the floor that my life changed forever.

Lots of people like to associate the floor with losing something and usually that something is your mind. However, if you think about whenever you lose anything after you've searched at eye level, eventually you're going to get frustrated enough to find yourself looking around on the floor. If you've ever made it to this point, you've had it! I had had it and was exhausted with everything. Being tired of hurt feelings, over all the issues, and mainly sick of not being able to get over whatever the world had done to me and what I had done to myself.

When you've lost yourself, it's the same reaction as to losing anything. Once you've been looking for so long, the focus is no longer on finding what's lost but shifts to who's at fault. After a while, you begin to feel like you didn't misplace anything but something's been taken from you. It becomes impossible to imagine that your everyday routine has created the possibility of losing something as precious as your mind.

I used to hear grown-ups speak about losing their minds when I was a kid, but I didn't know it was actually possible. I wasn't aware a nervous breakdown could really break you down to the point of finding yourself on the floor looking for something you didn't even realize you lost or until life lets you know abruptly you no longer had it.

Eventually, it's not about who did what or even about what was done. This is what I found by the time I got up off that floor. I started out a little angry, a little bitter, hurt, and confused, and most importantly a little misguided. But when I got up, I arose a little bit healed. When I landed on that floor I thought I was spiraling down, figuring it was the end. I was in the final stages of officially losing my mind and never finding it again.

I was questioning if I ever had it to begin with.

> I wrote until my pencil bled
> No ink allowed, just lead
> Almost time for lights out
> Silent night, but not really
> Hearing crying and screaming
> People begging for a healing
> I cried on the inside
> Because I felt that way too
> Praying for a miracle
> Hoping someone would save you
> Tired of the blues
> People here say they cry every day
> Some say they just write
> Funny I do the same
> Crazy, are we really
> Or is it just no one would listen
> Victims of lost souls and broken hearts
> Trying to find where do we go from here
> And how do we start

That question I mentioned earlier that I dread—Are you ok—I still wonder why people ask. That question alone is part of what got me here! Where is here exactly?

Well, it's several places technically; being alone, afraid, paranoid, depressed, and the good one—in a psych ward!

I have been asked if I was ok my entire life, but clearly, that question and my answer have gotten me nowhere. My issue is people always ask if you're ok at the lowest moments in your life. They never ask you on a payday if you're ok, or if you just got a bonus, nope still don't ask, or when you just booked that dream vacation and you guessed it, not a soul ever asked you if you were ok on those days. Nooo that question almost always gets asked on the worse possible days like you just found out your check is getting garnished, or your significant other just left you, or your car was repossessed. Yes, those are the wonderful days the entire world chooses to ask you if you're ok! Clearly, if I was ok I wouldn't be in this situation. On the other hand, when you do finally admit something's wrong people try to convince you, "it's going to be ok." Yes, my favorite line is, "Oh, it'll get better." Well, you know what; I am done lying to myself and allowing others to convince me that I'm ok when I'm really not.

For twenty-two of my twenty-six years, I had been abused in every way possible and I never received real treatment. I never sought justice nor got an apology, and I'm not just talking about my abusers. I never gave myself justice. I never even took the time to apologize to myself for not helping myself when I needed it. Instead, I allowed others and tried to convince myself that I was ok until I reached my breaking point. World, Stacey was not ok!

Nobody's Baby

    I have always loved the story of the *Titanic*. I realized my life was very much like that story. You see, I too was built up to have so much confidence. I thought I was strong enough to survive anything. However, "they" (whoever "they" were) were wrong. More importantly, I was wrong. There had been one very important differential factor—the *Titanic* was always just a ship; I was always just human and there was no escaping that.

    A lot of times, I got my warnings in life. I saw the troubling icebergs heading my way, but just like the story goes, I thought I could sustain the hits of coldness in the world. I assumed I was ready, believing I had been built for such things but we were all wrong.

    I understand now that I was always running full speed ahead into my trouble, always thinking I could take it. The *Titanic* had its sixteen compartments to store its pain and I had mine. Did anyone ever consider what would happen if those compartments got filled? Just like the water, my pain had reached the top and it spilled. Those compartments just kept filling and the pain continued to spill back and back and back until finally she broke, finally, she snapped!

    I had been a prisoner of my secrets for so long, I panicked when the truth came dangling its keys around my cell. The truth was always visiting me, trying to convince me to be free. Yet I didn't know how to be free. Everyone considered free was also usually considered crazy. I knew how to be crazy; I had been "crazy" all my life. However, I didn't know how to be free and crazy.

I bet by now you're saying, "Okay Stacey, we get you were hurting, but how did you get there? What about the guys you told us about so far, the relationships, the jobs, the dating? What led up to this?" Well, for starters, let's get one misconception clear. It is not only the little girls with disabilities who get mistreated. It's not only the very dark-skinned, overweight, not physically appealing little girls that bad things happen to. No one is exempt! This right here that I'm talking about, no one is exempt! Whether you've read the *Bible* or not and whether you believe or not, you will never even begin to understand the ruins of young Stacey unless you've read Second Samuel, chapter thirteen, the story of Tamar.

If you ever find yourself on the floor, you're onto something.

Yvonne Gurley

7 The Ruins

Did you read it? Second Samuel, chapter thirteen; have you read it yet? In case you haven't or never plan to, I'll remind you. You'll probably never fully understand the ruins of young Stacey if you don't. I'm not going to entertain you with the details of those horrible nights. I won't give you the rundown of all of Stacey's terrible days. I'm not going to tell a story that's been told over and over and over again. Adult Stacey refuses to through a "woe is me" party! I will, however, invite you to the truth.

    For some, it's a brother, sister, uncle, or aunt but for others, it's a cousin, friend, mother, father, or even a stranger. Then again, if you've ever lived through these experiences they all become strangers, even if we've known them your whole life. For some of us, it's a onetime thing. It happened just that once. For others, these events were more than just "events" or experiences. It was more than an occasion. This tragedy was actually life. Every single day, every single night, this was life, Stacey's life— MY LIFE! This is still life for some child out there. For some young boy or girl, at this very second, while you're reading this, this very circumstance is currently their life.

If you had the convenience of living with an abuser, you know that they hate you in the day and they love you at night. Other times they love you when everyone is around and they hate you every other time. None the less, it's all twisted.

The world puts so much focus on teaching adults how to cope with abuse, but if adults need all of these programs, how does the world think a kid is doing? Oh yeah, nobody ever asked! It seems like the world's way of dealing with battered children is to strip them from the family they know, put them in the system, which can be filled with more abuse, and then at eighteen send them on their way to figure it out. As I said, kids aren't talking to other kids about how they're being abused. It's every kid for him or herself.

For me, it seemed as though my first abuser cursed me like he left a sign on my head that said: "she's all yours." Every time I thought I was safe, every time I thought I was going to get some rest, that same demon would just hop into the next person's body almost everywhere I went. I would try to spend the night with friends or family thinking there would be peace, but that same perverted spirit would be right there waiting in the next person. There would be a friend's brother or father that looked at me weird; always something or someone waiting for their opportunity to take, too.

If you read Samuel, that chapter in that book I mentioned, you'd know that Stacey's main abuser went from loving her very much to extreme hate toward her. He'd physically abuse me in the day and sexually abuse me at night. Sometimes he'd allow his friends to take their turn as well. I have nothing more to say about that though; like I said it's all been heard and told before. However, there was one incident that completely destroyed what was left of Stacey's self-esteem. It was what changed the way I viewed myself from then on out, all the way until I was twenty-eight.

This nightmare called my life started when I was in elementary school and lasted until I was old enough to fight, or until I was old enough to be crazy, as I like to say. I was in junior high by the time this incident took place. By then, I had been taking years of abuse and never saying a word to anyone. How far gone do you think my mind was at that time? How was I supposed to be doing by that point? If you guessed I was suicidal, you're absolutely right. I always thought about getting out of here. No, I wasn't the slit-my-wrist type of kid. I just wanted out, so it was whatever "out" meant. I was more like "Please, God, don't let me wake up" type of suicidal. I had physically tried to commit suicide a few times before my teenage years started, but I had no idea how to actually accomplish it.

Are you ready? Are you ready for what put the final stamp on the beginnings of the ruins of Stacey? Here goes! My breaking point was eighth grade. I'd been sick—like always. Looking back, I question if my abuser had been poisoning me. After all, he'd done everything else he could do to destroy me. I had some kind of stomach bug, allegedly. I wasn't able to keep anything down. I could tell by the way he had been looking at me that night that I needed to muster up some strength to fight because it was going to be a fight; I didn't get very many nights off without one. Sure enough, I was right.

He came storming into my bedroom with his fist already balled up. However, I was ready this time. This time, I gave him all I had, and I got the best of him. He couldn't handle it. He stormed out of my room like the mad man he was. On the other hand, I was doing a small victory dance in my head.

My back was turned and as soon as I spun around, he had come back with a vengeance. He then gave me all that he had with just one punch. I was in so much shock in the instant, I felt no pain. However, due to the impact and my alleged stomach bug, I instantly started vomiting on the floor. I called out to my mother (that's right, I actually have one and most of the time she was home when all of my abuse occurred) but she stormed in pissed off from being disturbed by another one of our daily fights. She angrily asked what happened and as we each explained, her response to him was, "You didn't have to hit her so hard." She then turned to me and called me a female dog before stating, "You gonna clean that throw up off the floor. I'm not cleaning that up." Just like that, I was left alone in my mess as everyone else went on to their peaceful night's sleep, everyone except for me.

The next day I woke up to the worst headache one could imagine. I quickly ran to the mirror to see if my face was bruised though I swore I had a black eye. To my surprise, there was no black eye but what I saw was worse. Several blood vessels had burst in my left eye, which caused it to be completely red, not white, just red. Two weeks went by before the redness started to clear up.

Besides the bloodshot eye, I had massive headaches that seemed like they would not end. Over time, the headaches kept getting worse. I complained to my mother and older sister but they accused me of lying to get out of school.

On the days leading up to them getting tired of hearing my complaints, my vision seemed to be worsening. It started with just the headaches but then came double vision and then slowly it started to become hardly any vision at all. I couldn't even look up. To this day I still have a limit as to how far I can physically look up. By the time I was finally taken to the doctor, I witnessed the doctor pull my mother outside of the exam room and berate her. I didn't understand what was going on or why the doctor would even do such a thing. I wondered what he saw. I heard the doctor ask her what took her so long to bring me in. My mother began to cry as she tried to find a reasonable excuse—there wasn't one. There is never a valid reason for abuse and it took almost my entire twenties to realize that.

I had already been spiritually broken for most of my life already by that time but then I was told I was physically broken. As it turned out, the left side of my face had been shattered. All the bones around my left eye and left side of my nose were broken into tiny pieces. The bones were broken so badly that the doctors decided they would never heal. Ultimately, I ended up having surgery on my face to remove all of the broken bones and have them replaced with plastic.

My classmates began to speculate about why I had been missing from school and what happened. Teachers wondered, too. I made up a grand story that I had fainted and when I fainted I hit the corner of a dresser on my way down. Great story, huh? Even after all of this, still, my mother avoided me and my sister apologized for not believing something was really wrong. Other than that, nothing else was ever said or done in regard to that abuser or any other situation in that house.

I would eventually not just recover from this incident, but also from being a kid altogether. Though childhood should never be something you have to recover from, I did. I resented being a child because I never felt like I was a child; I would always identify more with my childhood friends' mothers than I did with my friends because I felt like they felt like me. The ones who were in bad relationships, the ones who were unhappy—I felt like my heart and spirits were closer to a grown woman who had already been through life's heartaches. However how they felt was how I already felt only as a kid, not an adult.

Whereas most children feel extremely uncomfortable around adults and don't want to be around their friends' parents, I was the opposite. I'd rather be around my friends' mothers than around my actual friends since I had the same concerns as the moms like paying bills or being mentally tired or being forced to have a sexual relationship I didn't want to have as a kid. I was going through a lot of things that most women don't have to deal with until they're adults and in a relationship with a family. I never opened up to my friends' mothers yet I felt this connection to them. Whether they were aware or not, the connections remained.

Due to the similarities I had with my friends' mothers, I developed a split personality. I created this version of me from what I thought a kid should be like. I sucked at being a kid because it was something I was always trying to do instead of just being me. I could never just be because I had to perform in one way or another for everyone. My friends knew a character, a version of me I created, however, that young Stacey my friends *thought* they knew was never me. I truly was the person I became when I was around my friends' parents. I know that sounds backward, but it's true. I felt relieved around adults. I had the freedom to be as mature as I wanted without getting the backlash from my friends such as "You're too serious. You don't know how to play." My sense of humor and imagination was different because I had adult problems. I was always myself around adults and different around other kids.

This made growing up very hard because I felt like I omitted a phase. The innocence and peace of being a child were not given to me—I skipped it! I didn't really want to be friends with my peers. I wanted adult friends because I felt akin to them—they were my true peers. I was conflicted for years. Even when I became an adult, I continued to clash and not relate to my peers. Was I ever immature? Yes! I was very childish, but not at the times I was supposed to be and it messed me up. I couldn't relate to my peers in certain phases of life. I skipped growing pains in so many areas of my life that by the time all of this would catch up to me, I would have made a mess of everything.

During my abuse, I kept telling myself, "You shouldn't be a kid right now." I waited for a grown-up to give me permission to be a kid yet nobody ever did. It wouldn't be until I got to my twenties when I finally gave myself permission to be immature yet, at the same time, permission to mature. In my twenties, I would like who I wanted to like no matter the dynamics or circumstances around me because most teenage girls don't care about those details. All I ever paid attention to was if a guy liked me and made me happy, that's as far as my thought process would go. I was off balance and I paid a heavy price for it, too. Nevertheless, I don't regret anything.

I'm glad I finally gave myself permission at some point to learn those lessons and go through those important growing pains I missed. I hate the fact that I waited so long but I'm grateful I didn't wait any longer. Am I a bad person to some people? Yes. Am I harshly judged by some people? Again, yes! Am I truly the person I displayed in my twenties? No!

I just needed to go through all the versions of me that I wasn't to get to the person I was truly meant to be.

8 Wounds and Scars

Just in case you're unaware of how it feels to be spiritually broken, I can tell you. It may not be an exact definition, but you will understand what it felt like for me.

Young Stacey spent most of her life trying to figure out where she was bleeding, why she was bleeding, and when and if the bleeding would ever stop. At one point, for a good chunk of my life, I got to the point where I stopped trying to find my wounds and only focused on covering them up. You can't resolve what you don't know the answer to, right? To go even further, how can you find the answer if you don't even know what to ask? You see, that's what it was like for me being broken all those years. It felt like I had this huge scar or some open wounds that just kept bleeding. People kept bringing my bleeding to my attention but they couldn't tell where the bleeding was coming from, and neither could I. All that everyone could see, all that I could see was that something was cracked and hemorrhaging but no one could find the traces of it to ever mend it and make it stop.

I got so tired of others noticing my scars with me that I decided to forgo trying to discover them anymore and concealed them instead. Just imagine this bizarre scenario because to me this is exactly what it felt like to be spiritually broken.

Was there more to my childhood? Was there anything else that contributed to young Stacey's demise? Of course, but like I said the story's been told before. Hopefully, I explained enough for you to understand her side because for the rest of Stacey's young adult life she'd spend it trying to live out everyone else's side of the story. She attempted to make someone else's truth her truth but, eventually, she realized that was a task no one could ever see to completion.

My abusers didn't want my story to be true, and honestly, neither did my family, friends, or anyone else who thought they knew me or what I was going through. No one wanted to be responsible for what my life had become; it was easier for everyone to pretend nothing ever happened and I was just dramatic. It was like the proverb of the three monkeys—see no evil, hear no evil, speak no evil.

On the other hand, I did everything I could to make it easier for me, too. I buried those memories deep down into the soil of my soul, hoping that burying such a seed would never result in any type of bloom.

I was wrong.

Something was growing on the inside of me, I just didn't know it. On that night of the incident that put the final stamp on my brokenness, I received an understanding. I thought surely—finally—something would be done. I thought this was it and at least one of my abusers would have to answer for what he'd done, but I was wrong. When nothing was done or even said about how broken I was, it proved to me that I truly was nobody's baby. I really didn't belong to this family and no one really loved me.

Nobody's Baby

I had felt that way all my life and after that happened it was confirmation. People go to war over a mistreated dog that's not even their pet, let alone a family member. I wasn't even given the rights of an animal. Anytime I tried to speak up or have a reaction to anything, I was always treated like I was overreacting or being dramatic. Any attempt to explain why I was behaving in such a way made everyone irritated and bothered. Basically, I was getting on their nerves because I kept "bringing that up." By "that" was an incident of my physical abuse and brokenness. I was the one living it every day—the nightmares, the paranoia, the anxiety, the physical, emotional, and spiritual scars, but *I* was getting on *their* nerves.

I had to face school, work, and events as a kid with all this baggage and do it sober! At least adults usually coped with something to allow them to get over it or to deal with it, but I was dealing with all of my shame, hurt, and embarrassment with nothing, and alone. When I was a teen, sex was the last thing I wanted to do and taking any type of drug or alcohol never crossed my mind. As far as Jesus was concerned, I stopped crying out to him the night my face got broken. I had decided he didn't love me either.

There's a certain level of disgrace and culpability that you carry when you've lived this type of life. You're not only embarrassed this happened to you, but you're also embarrassed for everybody else, too. I worried about what people would think and say about my mother for her lack of control and not doing anything when her child was being so blatantly abused. I cared what people would think about my other siblings for not doing anything either. How would people treat my abusers when they found out just what kind of monsters they really were? I felt guilty. I felt like I'd be ruining every one of their lives if I made a big deal about how they were destroying mine.

As I have explained, I felt so alone growing up. I always had plenty of friends but nothing ever cured my state of loneliness. We weren't a church-going family but somehow, I always knew there was a God. I never developed imaginary friends in my loneliness; instead, I'd always just talk to God. I'd cry myself to sleep sometimes just staying up all night talking to him. I never knew if he heard me or was truly listening. It wouldn't be until much later in life that I'd realize he had heard my every word. When I made the decision we would no longer speak, life got even lonelier for me and honestly, it got harder, too.

I became as awkward as a person could be. Without God's little whisper, I was always at lost for how to be, especially around people. It was always my mission not to stand out and be noticed yet the way I portrayed myself had the opposite effect. I was continually pointed out for trying not to be detected. It seemed as though I couldn't handle much, as almost everything was a trigger for me. However, it would be years before I even knew what triggers were or that a person could even have them. I was fragile. The average person most likely jumps and laughs when a person sneaks up on them in a playful manner. I, on the other opposite spectrum, immediately go into fight or flight mode. For many years, I found it very difficult to function in society. I had so many triggers that I wasn't even aware of, making much of what people did or said seem like some sort of threat or insult. Since I felt like I had no mother, I became my own mother and I did everything I could to defend the helpless little girl that lived inside me — the young adult Stacey.

So here we are. I'm summing up my childhood wounds and scars right here. I battled whether or not to give you all the graphic details of every single painful night of young Stacey's life but concluded you didn't need that, as some of you have lived it for yourselves. Not only that but after all these years, I'm still protective of them. I still care about other people's guilt and I still care about how my truth would make them feel. I'm not sure if feeling the need to protect them will ever go away. Yet, how do I tell my story accurately without bringing justice to all those involved? Plus, I didn't want you to focus on my pain or my abusers. Though I speak in great detail about it, it's actually not what this book is about.

I pray when my story is complete you will receive just what you need from it; maybe it's just entertainment, maybe my lesson is your lesson, or maybe, above everything else, I hope my story is a blessing.

It's far from over you know. There is so much more to tell. Eventually, I'd master wearing a mask throughout my life. I also had a lot of baggage I wasn't aware I was carrying. I had my whole life ahead of me and thought I left my luggage far behind; I didn't realize when I left them on the curb that I'd have some bags waiting on me somewhere that would eventually have to be unpacked.

Yvonne Gurley

She attempted to make someone else's truth her truth but, eventually, she realized that was a task no one could ever see to completion.

9 Things My Mother Taught Me

Look, I wish I had this big twist in my story. I wish I could tell you how things got so much better after I left my mother's house. If only I could say I met the love of my life and finally got everything I ever wanted, it would be more than inspiring. Unfortunately, that's not how it happened. I was battling many generational curses that I wasn't even aware of. Little did I know that my traumatic childhood was only the beginning. I would have many more things I'd have to survive.

In a nutshell, things didn't get better. For ten more years of my life, things remained in their dormant position. I wanted to make up something great so you could ride along this exciting road of adventure, but my story didn't go that way, and I'm sure some of yours didn't either. There was so much I thought about not sharing at all but I had a moment with myself. What if every little incident, conversation, or fight I left out was something you're going through or you've gone through? What if there is another young Stacey out there who needs me? Whether you can relate to every single word I've written, every chapter I've poured my heart into, I can't have you thinking you're the only one going through what you're going through.

Even if its addiction, being a single parent, or you knowingly or inadvertently dated

Yvonne Gurley

someone who was already taken by someone else, I realized I could not leave it out because what may seem trivial to others is a living nightmare for you, only it's called your life. So, it's my mission to show you that I'm just like you.

I was chasing joy! I thought I was chasing love, chasing money, success, you name it. However, now I know that I was always chasing joy! What are any of those things without it? Happiness is superficial, something you can fake. But joy, there ain't no faking joy. You either got it or you don't because joy comes from within you. I discovered I'd much rather have joy because in having it, I'll never have to pretend to be happy.

One day I'd learn that I'd rather have joy than happiness so I never had to pretend to be happy. You see, my mother did the same thing, and my sisters, too. Heck, everyone I knew was chasing joy but not one of us knew we were chasing it. Now that I'm no longer on that wild goose chase, I would tell young Stacey to learn to find joy no matter who you are or where you are or the situation. Joy must not be dependent upon your status, position, or location. If your joy is reliant upon those things you will never have it or it will always be temporary.

Pray! Pray because it really works and because you really need it. No matter how big or small the prayer is just say something. Talk to God even if you don't know what to say. Heck, tell him that! Tell him when you don't know. Be grateful, regardless of how you feel your life should be going—be grateful!

My battles were not just for me. I'd like to think that what I learned is what my daughter will master! My heart almost broke the day I saw all my flaws in her face and heard them in her voice. It kept me up all night. I thought I was up to worry but I wasn't; I was up to pray, to learn. I was up so my daughter and you won't have to be.

My battles or my lessons—I had to decide. *You* have to decide! You see, I've had the attitude of my battles, my hurt, my pain, my sorrow, yet I was supposed to have the mindset of my lessons, my blessings, my triumphs, and my victories! Only, I didn't have this thought process because at a very young age I learned how to worry and complain. I was educated on how to worry because it was what my mother taught me. My mother had gone through a lot; I have been through a lot. I've experienced pain that some people who live to see eighty never see. I'm not complaining though, I'm explaining.

My mother was a single parent of four and I was the youngest. I'm not sure if she would do this on purpose but she would leave eviction and shut off notices out so that we could see. I was a kid in class worrying about bills my mother couldn't pay, nor could I. I worried if we got put out of our house where we were going to stay. I spent my days, not thinking like a kid about math or recess or art, but about going home to listen to my mother on the phone arguing about bills and money. My mother taught me how to worry but she didn't teach me how to pray. I assume it's because she didn't know how.

Since my mother had the mindset of my trials and not my triumphs, my sisters and I repeated a lot of her mistakes, mistakes that should have been life lessons to avoid. We heard about what she went through but heard nothing about what she learned. She didn't teach us the results of her mistakes; instead, she taught us the complaints. As a result, we carried all of her flaws.

I refused to repeat the cycle. I was never supposed to suffer all that I did, but my daughter was *not* going to live a repeat of my life.

Just when I was about to decide to stay up all night worrying about my daughter being just like me, God reminded me he never sleeps. There's never a reason to be up all night worrying about anything. If you're up worrying and not praying, you may as well just go back to sleep because the two have the same result.

I'm teaching my daughter to give it to God! I encourage you too to give it to Jesus! Change your mind set. Focus and teach what you've learned instead of always telling what you've been through. Stop complaining and start explaining. Reflect and learn instead of crashing and burning!

The good news is you made it, I made it! Whatever your "it" is you survived! Don't teach your kids' life is hard without teaching them they can make it! Now when my daughter reads over "Things My Mother Taught Me," her story will be different and knowing that gives me the ability to thank God for this lesson!

That thing I spent a decade chasing turned out to be God. Joy is something that only he can give you. I didn't know this. I tried to find it in every guy I ever dated, every job I ever worked, every friendship I had, and I even tried to find joy in my addiction. Then again, I looked for joy in the thrill of chasing joy—now that is something! Nonetheless, when I found myself eighteen and in my first hard place as an adult, I landed on the first sign of joy I thought I saw. Get ready, it's Byron again!

I discovered I'd much rather have joy because in having it, I'll never have to pretend to be happy.

Yvonne Gurley

10 Against My Better Judgement

You pay for what you don't know—truly. When I left my mother's house, I thought I knew something, as we all do. The fact that I even let Byron in my life proved I knew nothing at all.

Judgment—what's that? I had very poor judgment. I once told you I thought Byron was a "good guy, a Godfearing, family man" to be exact. However, how could he possibly be any of those things if he came for me? In case you forgot, Byron was twenty-five and married with three children when eighteen-year-old Stacey met him. He also had quite a few vices, the kind that made a person lose more than time or money; his vices were the kind of habits that would make a young girl like Stacey lose herself.

One would have thought I would have run for the hills. Heck, anyone with any sense at all would have never found themselves in this period. I fell for the first sign of what I thought was love and a chance at being a part of a real family. Not only that, but I also fell into the same situation that I so harshly judged my mother for. Aside from childhood abuse, this was another generational curse. My mother, like her mother before her, dated married men and birthed their children. My mother didn't know her mother's story and I didn't know my mother's; had I been warned; someone could have prayed for me or I could have been given the opportunity to pray for myself. How could I have been prepared for this curse when it came knocking at my door if no one ever told me not to open it.

My mistreatment was always swept under the rug when I was growing up so, honestly, it didn't take much for me to see the "good" in bad things or bad people. You see, my mother wasn't always cursing me out; occasionally, she was nice but it didn't last very long. I only experienced two versions of my mom. She was the sweetest person in the world when she had her pills or she was your typical angry aggressive addict without her fix.

When good treatment is not consistent in a child's life, their first impression of what love is can be distorted; by the time the child becomes an adult, his or her gage for love is going to be off kilter. You learn to overlook when someone is mistreating you because it doesn't seem like it's so bad. I fell for flowers and a few kind words while I was mourning. I fell for being comforted in my time of need. How easy, how simple was it for a guy like Byron to make an impression!

I never knew a successful relationship or marriage. Everyone I knew and everyone around me all had failed relationships. I used to look at my friends' parents but as the years went by their imperfections were exposed and I found myself with no examples at all. After my mother's failed attempts at love, she settled throughout my childhood with men already claimed by other women. My sisters and I would follow down the same paths. With this example in my life, I ended up despising my mother. I'd be filled with rage every time I saw a man coming in through the back door. I vowed I would never allow such a thing, however, even though no one ever physically came through any back door of mine, they did come through in other ways.

Byron was full of it from the very beginning. There were more than red flags to warn me—there were sirens, bull horns, and alarms going off, yet I ignored them all. I was just grateful to not wake up to someone spitting in my face while I attempted to make myself breakfast. I was glad I wasn't paying for someone else's bad day by being yelled at or physically beaten. Shucks, all Byron had to do was not spit on me, beat me, or verbally abuse me and in my mind, it made him a good guy.

What that Stacey didn't know was there was another type of abuse. As if I could take any more, young Stacey was about to find out that emotional abuse has just as powerful as the hardest punch she ever endured. Emotional abuse can leave your soul with a hole the size of a twelve-gauge shotgun shot at close range.

From the beginning, Byron was cheating, lying, smoking, drinking, and some other things I didn't know were real addictions. However, I ignored all of these things because my measurement of good treatment was nonexistent. I was nineteen and in college, so of course, I didn't think there was anything wrong with smoking marijuana, having drinks with friends, or partying until the wee hours. I didn't see anything wrong with it until I was no longer invited. Yeah, that coworker fun came to an abrupt end.

Byron ended up losing his job at the law firm not long after I did. He hit me with some phony excuse which I later found out was a lie. He claimed that one of the lawyers found cocaine on the floor outside of the bathroom and demanded a random drug test from everybody. Because Byron was a heavy marijuana smoker, he was quickly let go of his position. It never dawned on me that there was a possibility the cocaine was Byron's. It would be years before I would ever come to the conclusion of his heavy use of cocaine and pills.

I used to be so bitter, so angry with Byron, and with my mother, and with my entire family. I blamed my family for not preparing me for him and for life as a whole. Somebody should have warned me. Someone should have protected me. For a long time, I made everyone responsible for my broken heart.

After I left my family and settled in with Byron, I truly held him accountable for the care of my already broken heart. How foolish was I? How immature and lost was I to have done such a thing? I wanted Byron to save me but he couldn't because he needing saving too.

Yvonne Gurley

There are two ways to look at what I'm about to share with you. You can say Byron put Stacey through so much, or you can say Stacey put Stacey through so much. I battled with that thought for a long time. It's a cold world out there, and it's even colder when you're convinced, you're nobody's baby. You'll do almost anything to become somebody's person.

You have no line of defense for what you don't know is coming.

11 Sloppy Seconds

By the time I was twenty, the glamour of Byron and the dream of belonging to a loving family had long worn off. I had mourned as much as I possibly could over my friend and my father. I had also walked into something I wasn't grown enough for, wasn't ready for. I felt stuck.

Just a year and a half had gone by since the start of my relationship with Byron and he had managed to move in and lose several jobs along the way. He was very irresponsible. Later on down the line, he loved to take credit and say he moved me from my tiny one-bedroom apartment into a lavish three-bedroom upscale apartment that was also roomy enough for him and his three kids. Granted he had gotten a better paying job that enabled us to move, but he also lost that good job and I ended up being responsible for keeping us in that apartment, which I never needed.

By that time, I was tired of the lying and cheating, too. Don't worry, the stealing comes later. A friend had advised me she saw his profile on an online dating site. I quickly got on the site and created a fake profile just to see what she saw. I even gave him the benefit of the doubt and defended him, stating it was probably an old profile. Why do women do this? Someone, please tell me why we defend those that don't need to be defended. Anyway, I tested the waters. I used this fake profile as bait to see if he would actually try to talk to me. Lo and behold, he bit with no hesitation. To this day he never found out I had conversed with him for months. Did I mention the women who were calling our home phone? Yes, at that time people still had house phones or landlines. On one particular day after another phone call, I had my things ready to go to leave Byron. Suddenly, he came running to the door begging and pleading for me to stay, he even broke down crying. This did something to me. At that moment, I realized I had never seen a man cry before. I was in such shock by how it made me feel I stupidly put my bags down and stayed. *I actually stayed.* Looking back, I know that young Stacey wasn't seeing a man cry but she was seeing a boy cry.

Yvonne Gurley

No, things did not change after that; if anything they got worse. I began to sink into a deeper depression as my high school friends were raving about college life, parties, and dating; meanwhile, I was stuck in the house every weekend with three kids who weren't mine. Byron didn't miss a beat, however. He was gone with the wind every weekend his kids came over.

During that time, I desperately needed something to love and I needed something to love me back. So, I clung to the kids. I would look forward to them coming and our time together. I'm the youngest and always wondered what it would be like if I had little sisters. Starting out, I couldn't see them as stepchildren but truly like little sisters. I played with them, polished their nails, and combed their hair. Honestly, the kids had clung to me just as much as I clung to them considering it was a difficult time for them as well.

Nobody's Baby

Byron could tell I was growing weary again so his master plan to ensure my staying for good was to impregnate me. I had always believed I couldn't have children, as my gynecologist told me during my first pap smear; due to the curve of my pelvis and all the damage from being sexually abused as a child, I could not have one of my own. I still kept birth control pills on me and treated them like the morning-after pills, taking two or three pills every time I thought it was a possibility of something.

One night Byron convinced me I really didn't need to take those pills because it was dangerous to my body to take them the way I had been. Well, I listened. I was beyond submissive; I was stupid and very naïve. Low and behold, a few weeks later I find out I was pregnant. If I didn't already feel trapped, I really felt imprisoned then. I really couldn't leave and a sense of doom washed over me.

Byron and his family were extremely excited as they were hoping for a boy since he already had three girls. I'll never forget the day we found out about my daughter. I saw the light in Byron's eyes quickly fade. He became even more disconnected than he already was and so did his family. During my pregnancy, women continued calling and his activity on his dating sites persisted. He eventually moved on from dating sites and began chatting with women on porn sites as well. I couldn't use our home computer without receiving a chat message from another woman. I was disgusted and hopeless all at the same time.

Not long after my daughter was born, Byron managed to lose another job. I would come home from work to a houseful of marijuana smoke and a group of his friends who had spent the entire day playing video games, smoking, drinking, and God only knows what else. I was miserable. My house would always be a mess; there'd be a sink full of dishes, baskets of clothes, and unopened bills piling up for me to pay. We were operating with one vehicle, so of course, Byron would drop me off at work and, if I was lucky, he'd pick me up on time. A lot of days I'd end up having to catch a ride from coworkers after realizing Byron was not going to show up at all. Then I'd come home to my car sitting right outside as he and his friends were high as a kite. As if that wasn't bad enough, his response would be "my bad" when I came through the door.

I had no respect in my own home from Byron or his family. Even the kids that I once so dearly loved began to show little to no respect for me. I began to feel the little bit of what was left of me fade into the darkness. But we faked it, and we faked it well. I never let anyone know, not even my closest friends, exactly what I was enduring day in and day out. Thanks to my childhood, I was already a master of deception. I did what I knew how to do—suffer alone.

When I first started dating Byron I really thought I had someone special. However, I didn't steal some other woman's prize, I got her sloppy seconds! Having been on both sides of this fence I'd like to speak to any of the young Stacey's out there and just say you're not winning! No matter what side of the fence you're on, nobody's winning. Whether you're the one that's being cheated on or the one he's cheating with, you're not winning. Both of you are getting sloppy seconds and I'd like to encourage you to know that you're both worth so much more than that!

I had also walked into something I wasn't grown enough for, wasn't ready for.

I felt stuck.

12 Addicted

The emotional abuse from my relationship sent me on a downward spiral. I began to do what some would refer to as "act out." I discovered all of this new pain was triggering my old pain from my childhood that I thought I had so deeply buried. I began to have panic attacks and snap on people. I was a force to be reckoned with. Byron convinced me that I was going through postpartum depression. My doctor prescribed me my first antidepressants and I checked the heck out of there—for seven whole years. I was excited. I never knew there was such a thing that could seemingly numb all my pain. I thought my pills were my cure.

Still, the level of disrespect I was receiving was out of control. Nonetheless, I continued to fake my happy, perfect life with Byron in our lavish apartment. I even decided to attempt to go back to college. I figured my days of being a writer and studying journalism and broadcasting were more than over. I had already been working in insurance and healthcare for quite some time, so I decided to go to school for medical coding, as during the time the TV was flooded with commercials for this new, high demand medical field. I was excited. Even though it was an online class, it gave me a little light that, despite my heartache, I was still bettering myself.

My light was dimmed fairly quickly as Byron lost another job. That's when he came to me desperate with this new business plan that was supposedly really going to make things better for us. At first, I turned his plan down. I turned it down several times. If you think he couldn't make my life any more hellish than it already was, think again. This man did everything he could to make things miserable for me at home until I eventually gave in. I stupidly handed Byron over my entire student refund check. Want to know what his big plan was? He and his want-to-be gangster cousin took my money and bought a large number of ecstasy pills and decided they were going to try their hands at being drug dealers. Yeah, two guys who grew up with both parents in their middleclass home decided that was where they wanted to go in life, and at my expense.

I was so busy with going to work during the day and school and being a mom when I got home that I would give Byron the money to pay the bills. I'd eventually come home from work to a padlock on the door to my beautiful apartment and a note that said the rent had not been paid in three months. I was devastated. They would let me in only to find out my lights had been turned off too because that hadn't been paid either. You guessed it, Byron had been hiding the notices of no or late payment. The pills he was supposed to be selling were not sold; instead, Byron, his cousin, and his friends had a field day and took them all. Obviously, we were forced to move out, as our apartment was already expensive so getting behind in an amount of rent like that you don't have any other choice but to leave.

While I was going through all of this in my personal life, I had quite a few people who attempted to be my friend. These women were truly good to me and some of the best experiences of friendships I ever had to this date. However, I could not be a friend back. I had just turned twenty during all of this. I was young and so very lost, not to mention I was embarrassed. I didn't know how to tell these women that I was this stupid. I couldn't confess that this was my life. They saw me all dressed up at work and the fake smile I put on my face and had no clue about my life when I walked out of those company doors every day. I'm certain I left a bad taste in all of their mouths as I was in no position to be a good friend back.

Not only did I lose my apartment, but I also suffered another layoff. Once again, I dropped out of school and was forced to move in with my mother as Byron moved in with his parents. I never once explained to my friends what happened. I just slowly faded myself out of their lives forever. Every now and then I run into some of them or have tried to befriend them on Facebook, but they decline or do not respond. I don't blame them. They were there for me and did so much for me and I gave them nothing in return. I couldn't though, I didn't know how. I had been hiding my pain all my life and I wasn't about to start talking.

Yvonne Gurley

Being back under my mother's roof ate away at me every single day. We didn't get along, though we never did. I had no respect for her and felt abandoned in more ways than one. I had already felt abandoned as a child, but she even treated me that way as an adult, too. During my pregnancy, I did not receive support from her. If anything, when we did speak it always led to a cussing battle and hanging up in each other's face. I was left to figure out how to be a mother all on my own. I would have to ask my co-workers questions. The first time I woke up to breast milk all over the sheets I thought I was dying. I knew nothing about raising a child. I never babysat growing up. I was so lost. I knew I wasn't going to last too long in my mother's tiny one-bedroom apartment with her.

Byron managed to get himself arrested and receive his first drug charges. His mother accused me of not being supportive and not caring because I did not go to the court date. She didn't consider the fact that my only car was impounded thanks to her son and I was stuck with a newborn baby alone.

During his court battles, I went through my own process of getting unemployment and finding another place for me and my daughter. I couldn't take another month in my mother's presence. As Byron was dealing with his charges, I had gotten my car back and paid the deposit on a small two-bedroom apartment back in my hometown, not too far from my mother's place. My unemployment checks had started rolling in so I was able to start the process of getting back on my feet.

Nobody's Baby

Byron was ecstatic. He found his way from his parents' house and moved right in with me and our daughter. His other three kids fell right back into the routine of being dumped off on me every weekend too. By then, I couldn't see myself getting off my antidepressants any time soon. I fell into a routine of waking up, taking my pills, and accepting whatever horror the day would bring thanks to Byron and his addiction. Our previously luxury apartment complex generously gave an opportunity for us to still come by and get our things even though the apartment had been padlocked. Byron and his cousin went to go move everything out. Well, to my surprise, I got my furniture and Byron managed to get all of his things, however, all of my clothes, shoes, and purses did not make it. My daughter's piggy bank didn't make it either. These things mysteriously just disappeared.

I was so numb by that point; I could no longer feel the effects of whatever Byron did to me, whatever I did to me by staying. Byron would begin to accumulate several more drug-related charges, which ultimately resulted in my car being taken away permanently by the police. Even though this was the start of my addiction, I'm almost positive I would have died from a broken heart, as I had nothing left inside me, had I not been on any medication at all. I don't think I even felt like I was still a person anymore. I had completely isolated myself, had no friends at all, and talking to the family was never an option. I became this shell that existed, not living, only existing.

Yvonne Gurley

I'd find out years later that his marijuana, porn, sex, and pill addiction had added another friend to the list—cocaine. I believed he had always experimented but he became a full-blown cocaine addict. I never saw him do it, ever, but once I learned about the signs of this drug use, I was able to pinpoint about the time where this neverending cold and allergy season began. Things seemed to only be getting worse and worse. On one night, in particular, he openly admitted to being high off of cocaine. He had come in extremely late, about two or three in the morning which was his norm, and I thought he was drunk as he reeked of alcohol and marijuana. Now let me just say that he always reeked, but this time the smell was worse than usual. He came in and woke me up out of my sleep to attempt to have sex with me. Now I had long been done in that department with him; the thrill was more than gone, the thrill died! I wasn't just this broken little girl mourning the loss of a friend in search of somebody to love her. I was angry, bitter, numb, and over it. Anyway, the fact he was even attempting to wake me up with this pissed me off to the max. When I tell you we fought, it was a fight. He wasn't only trying to have sex with me, but he was trying to force anal on me. All of my triggers went off. I gave him all I had that night and I didn't act upon the rage I felt inside. I mean it; I'm really surprised because of how much was brewing inside of me.

The next day, when he finally decided to join the rest of the world and wake up, he wanted to start explaining and crying and admitting to doing cocaine. He made it seem like it was his first time trying it, but it was not his first rodeo. I didn't give two flips about his tears because by that point Byron was always crying about something. I was over that, too. I simply took my pills and tuned him out with our daughter's beautiful face.

She was truly beautiful, and I got lost looking at her. Staring at her and seeing her smile drowned the world out for me. When my pills weren't enough, she was enough. She's the reason why, at first, I took the pills as prescribed for the first few years I was on them. Being on unemployment allowed me to spend all my days with her. She made everything that was wrong in my life right when I looked at her. She was and will always be my everything. She was my miracle that I thought I could never have. She's my right thing! I was twenty when I had her. I'm now thirty and I've yet to have any more children, for reasons unknown to me.

My daughter is my walking, talking, breathing grace in the flesh! I can never say I don't know grace because of her.

13 The Blues

I know, I know, how dare I name this chapter "The Blues." I was way past the blues, right? However, I had the blues on top of my depression when Byron proposed to me. Yep, he proposed.

You see, he had learned about a crime that had been committed from a friend of his when they were guy chatting. First of all, no one ever expects friends to go tip off the cops after a conversation like that, but it's exactly what Byron did. He didn't do it because he was being a Good Samaritan or anything like that. He did it because he had learned the police were offering money to anyone who would provide information on the case. I'll never know the exact amount he was paid for this information, as of course, he did not share that with me. I knew nothing about the case or the crime I just knew that this was something he had done and was the way my ring was purchased.

He took himself down to a local pawn shop and let his mother pick out my ring. Now his mother picked out a ring that would have been nice for her; the style was dated and I hated it with a passion. His idea of proposing to me was taking me to the parking lot of my old one-bedroom apartment and saying, "Stacey man, would you marry me, man?" I wish I was kidding and I promise this is not for entertainment purposes, that's really how he proposed. There was no getting on one knee or any of that. We just pulled up in the parking lot; he stopped the car and made that horrible statement. I immediately start crying, and I mean I was crying hard. My pills weren't strong enough to take on what I was feeling at that moment.

What was the happiest and most dreamed about moment for most women was one of the worse moments in my life. I had developed so much hate in my heart towards him and so much bitterness and resentment, all I could do was cry. By the way, he proposed, he didn't love me either. He called me "man." He always called me man or dude as we did not use terms of endearment whatsoever. He used me. He used me as an escape from his wife, as an excuse for their divorce, and to attempt to have a son. I later found out his desire for a son was a major problem in his previous marriage, as his wife did not want to try for any more children after already having two, which was when he turned to me. When I too had a girl, he completely lost interest.

I used him, too, to be honest. The broken little high school graduate took the first sign of what she thought was real love and she didn't care where it came from or how she got it. She was broken, hurt, and lonely, so she accepted every form of comfort she could find.

Nobody's Baby

Byron and I were both unhappy and I guess one could say our misery might have been something we both deserved, giving the conditions by which we met. Wrong is wrong no matter if you know better or not. It doesn't matter if you're broken or not. There is no excuse for it and it took me a long time to accept that hard truth, though I don't think he has even to this day. I still believe Byron still hasn't realized exactly the damage he's done to himself, to his children, to me or his previous wife and mother of his other children.

Nevertheless, back to the proposal, he had the audacity to get upset with me for crying. Who wouldn't cry in my position? He was all upset fussing at me and said, "Now I have to lie to my friends and family about how you responded. Everybody knew I was going to propose to you today and you messed it up with your crying." So, I did what I knew to do—I put on a happy face and made my post on Facebook about being engaged to look like I was thrilled, and I contacted all of my family and told them. Everyone was so happy, everyone but me.

I felt like that ring sealed my fate to a lifetime of bondage with him. Having a family for my daughter meant everything to me. I had long been over being a part of a family for myself and was now staying and pretending in the relationship for my daughter. There was no way I was going to let her grow up in a home without both parents. I couldn't let her grow up without a relationship with her father. It was too risky; I didn't want her to be anything like me or any other fatherless girls I grew up with who made similar mistakes. So, I continued to take my pills, I wore the ring, and I sported a smile. Byron told his lies about my reaction and we were all good on the outside. I was good at faking it but Byron taught me how to master it. No one knew I was suffering so much inside.

My ring wasn't the only thing he bought with his tattle tale money. He also purchased a Cadillac from an ophthalmologist who had it for sale in the lot of his office. He paid for it in cash and then bought a new gaming system and games. He also took me shopping, in an attempt to make up for all of the clothes and shoes I had lost. I didn't nearly get back the number of clothes and shoes I had lost. He also bought dolls for me. I had been a Barbie doll collector, like the ones you can't buy at your local store but must be ordered. I had lost some of them too, so he bought a few that he could find. You see, all my life I dreamed I would one day have a baby girl so I managed to save these dolls, as well as all my favorite stuff animals and a few other things I deemed important to pass down to her. I was a collector of Beanie Babies as well. In one of the many cruel acts by Byron's other children, all of the tags were ripped off of my Beanie Babies, which would make them worthless. Those were never replaced.

Still, with all of this, I monstered up the strength to give the school a try as my daughter was getting older. I enrolled in another program for medical coding. While I was working on that, I also got my pharmacy tech license as well as a nursing assistant. I fell so in love with the medical field I wanted to eventually go to school to be a circulatory nurse and work in surgery. I had come up with this plan that I would first go on to school to be a surgery technician and then move on to a surgical nurse. While in school my instructors had so much faith in me and encouraged me that I could go further in medicine. While I was at school, my hopes were so high and for a moment I actually believed I could do all those things, but reality always sat in when I got home.

 I remember one day as I was coming home from school and pulling up to our apartment I saw the most popular guy from grade school. It was Wolf! He never finished school as he dropped out. There were so many rumors as to what he had decided to do with his life after dropping out. Despite the rumors, he was still so dreamy. I hadn't seen him in years by then, probably since I was in the ninth grade. This guy wasn't just your average handsome or good-looking dude. This man was pretty, as in beautiful. He's the type of good-looking that makes you freeze in your steps and just stop whatever you're doing, thinking, or talking about. There was something about his eyes. I had met dozens of guys with all sorts of eye colors but there was something special about his green eyes. If one ever had the privilege of making eye contact with him, his gaze would hold you as if you were face to face with a wolf but without the fear. There was something about his eyes that were different. He had flawless skin too; not a scratch or a bruise or a bump anywhere on him. He also had the most perfectly placed mole right above his top lip. His hair was as wavy as wavy could get. He was so handsome that even if light skinned black men aren't your type, he would be your type. He was fine no matter what your preference was. Did I mention he had dimples? In a jokingly manner it's like, "Dang God, you gave him dimples too!"

Anyway, I was getting out the car and as I began to walk, I looked up and there he was looking down at me from the balcony. My eyes met his and he spoke to me. I don't think I ever wanted to teleport so bad in my life. I answered him back and quickly ran to my apartment, embarrassed as to how I turned out and what condition I was in. I looked nothing like I did in school. After that, I would see him quite often, as he lived in the same building, but I made it a point for him to never see me. I was ashamed of myself and I was certainly ashamed of Byron.

Byron was still not working though he was enjoying his tattle tale money. You would think he would have paid off the many fines he racked up with drug charges but no, he didn't. All the rest of his money went to him and his friends getting high as they could stand. He bought nothing of real value and nothing that could assist in changing his life for the better. All that money did was allow him to nosedive into cocaine and ecstasy pills deeper than he had ever gone.

My hopes and dreams of medicine were always crushed the moment I walked in the door. Not only was I not going to be this famous writer, but I also wasn't going to be a nurse either. Despite it all, I managed to complete all of my vocational programs and went back to work. I was working in the pharmacy as well as the insurance company I was originally laid off from when I was eighteen. In an effort to save my family, I moved back to the city and out of my small hometown. In my mind, I blamed the town on Byron's lack of motivation and thought maybe we just needed a fresh start.

My daughter and I moved in with my oldest sister. We slept on the floor of her den. Byron went back to his parents' house. I stayed with my sister to save money as long as I could stand. You see, my sister was also pretty damaged from our childhood and I could not live with the residue from her untreated trauma. It was too much for me. Desperate to get off my sister's floor I jumped on the chance to be independent again and so, I found a house. This house was everything I wanted at the time. We hadn't had three bedrooms since the luxury apartment. Our street was called Sunnydale and I thought living on a street called Sunnydale life could not get any better. How could I not find happiness?

My daughter was going to have her own room and the girls would have theirs. By then, I had separated myself from any attachments I may have had in the past to Byron's other three kids. As they got older, they grew to be so disrespectful to me I just tuned them out when they came on the weekends. I no longer played with them, as our fun times had long been over and I was no longer nineteen. I wanted to be as far away in my mind as possible when they came. They also accused me of abuse, telling their mother and Byron's family every chance they got. No matter what I did or didn't do I defended myself against them, as Byron would always leave when they came over.

It seemed as though I was on trial for my life every day. I found myself explaining myself all the time. Byron knew nothing about trauma, abuse, or anything as he lived a quite sheltered life. He hadn't really gone through anything. Everything I said or did was referred to as crazy. I tried to open up to Byron about my traumatic childhood since I suffered from nightmares and would be quite violent in my sleep. I was still having panic attacks and could barely go into a store without having one. He tried to get an understanding from my family of me but my family had convinced him that I was just crazy and dramatic whenever I mentioned the truth about anything. So, when I would catch him lying, he joined in on their game of convincing me I was crazy and overreacting to everything. To all of them, I was crazy Stacey. I was crazy for laughing, crazy for crying, crazy for having an opinion, crazy for speaking the truth—I was crazy for feeling anything at all!

I was tired of explaining myself to everyone around me. I was so, so tired. I hadn't been this tired since I was a kid. I didn't want to feel anything anymore. I was done following the instructions of my prescriptions. They were no longer strong enough. I got tired of switching from this medicine to that medicine, this dosage to that dosage. So anytime I ever felt anything, I popped a pill. I didn't care if I was happy, sad, or mad; every emotion caused me to take a pill because I didn't want to feel any of it. I knew I couldn't kill myself physically, so I killed myself emotionally instead.

I was coherent just enough to function on a job, just enough to not die.

Yvonne Gurley

14 Circumstantial Love

I barely managed to get through training when I started back at my old job with the insurance company. I was high as a kite every single day. I looked forward to going to work; anything that got me away from my life at home gave me something to look forward to. I had nothing outside of work and Byron. I was like a prisoner who got work release every day and had to report back to prison after the job was over every night.

Work was the only time I was ever exposed to anyone outside of my home at that point. I still had no friends as I refused to let anyone get close to me. Work was the only time I witnessed how the rest of the world was carrying on.

By then, Byron and I had been together for seven years. My daughter was two and a half and I was twentyfour. Time had been passing and as the years went by, I hadn't noticed just how much time had passed at all. The years all seemed to just blur together. In my mind, mentally, I was still eighteen. Life was happening but I never matured passed eighteen, as I had been in a bubble with my life with Byron. Our engagement, if you want to call it that, had been dragged out. Every year our date would come up and I would always say I needed more time. I never needed more time; I needed away from him and my entire life with him. At one point, I actually planned a wedding and tried on dresses in my effort to fake my happiness with my family. I'll never forget Byron's mother saying to me, "I don't know what you're doing all of that for, planning a wedding and all. If you have a wedding there will not be anyone from Byron's side of the family who will attend." Yep, somehow, I was the sole blame of how Byron's life was turning out. His life was all my fault. By then Byron had been in and out of jail several times and had so many drug charges that it seemed impossible for him to get a job anywhere. So, I continued to carry the weight of our family, if you can even call it a family.

At work, I mostly stayed to myself. I tried as hard as I could to blend into the background. Even though none of our jobs required us to be on the phone, it was still a call center environment with the cubicles and such. Work almost felt like high school all over again. You had your cliques of the popular and the not so popular crowds. Just like it was for me in high school, trying to not stand out put a spotlight on me. It made people curious. Who was the girl who just came to work and actually just worked? Whenever anyone tried to have a conversation with me, I'd give short, vague answers, which made it obvious I didn't want to be bothered.

There was this one girl though, Jamaica, who wouldn't give up. Maybe she saw herself in me. She could see right through me, as I would later find out she was high on pills, too, just like me. We would spend our lunch breaks talking about how miserable we were. She told me she felt like she was living a nightmare—exactly how I felt every

Nobody's Baby

day. We became inseparable as no one at the time knew me quite as she did. She was the first person I ever let into my real pain.

On the weekends, Byron would take the only car we had, my Camry, and leave early in the morning before I could wake up or really late at night. He had run that Cadillac he bought from the optometrist into the ground by now. He knew once I took my pills I'd be out for quite a while. He would stay out the entire weekend, leaving me and my daughter in the house with no food or anything and without a care in the world from him.

Jamaica was the only person I trusted at the time. I'd call her and she comes to our rescue on the weekends to get us out of the house. She'd even take us to get something to eat. Our friendship really lightened the load I was carrying and I was letting some of that heat out that had been brewing inside me for so many years. She let her steam out, too. Neither of us did much outside of our family lives and we began to make time to have moments to ourselves.

Jamaica loved going to the casino, so I would join her. I was never into gambling but I didn't care. We used to say we were Thelma and Louise. We'd pop our pills and hit the road—it was the most happiness I had felt in I didn't know how long. Our daughters were just a year apart and we allowed them to play and do activities together as often as we could. We were so proud to have such beautiful girls that we began to let them model together and start training for gymnastics, too.

Jamaica and I had gotten so close we began to refer to each other as sisters. She was seven years older than me and, at the time, she was like a big sister; she was always coming to my rescue as she knew and understood the depths of my pain. Because of her, I had slowly begun to open up to my actual sisters about what I was going through, as they had no idea. I faked my relationship with Byron so well, no one had a clue. I even went as far as getting Valentine's Day cards made with our family photo on it. We had all the holiday dinners at my house in which I faked a happy, loving family to perfection. My sisters couldn't believe the truths I was telling them. I also found out they were suffering just as much as me, as both of my sisters were also in relationships with addicts and going through their own abuse as well. One of my sisters proclaimed, "We all have our own personal hells we live in," and she was right. We were all in this together yet alone at the same time. We couldn't help each other, not even a little bit.

 I'd grow to learn the hard way that some relationships are circumstantial, and some friendships are too. The circumstances of mine and Byron's relationship created an opportunity for Jamaica and me to bond. We became friends over misery. My sisters and I talked because of misery and nothing more. This wasn't healthy or helpful at all, except, I thought it was. Just like I did when I was eighteen, I was back to hopes of love, family, and comfort. And just like then, I thought I had found it. In seven years, I hadn't grown at all and I learned nothing from my relationship with Byron except for how to survive, how to lie, and how to get high. Though I never tried any street drugs beyond marijuana, I was just as much an addict as

Byron, but I couldn't see it. I made the mistake of thinking

I was better than him because my pills were prescribed to me and I was just treating an illness. In some ways I was, but in other ways, I was only feeding the many demons I had let get inside of me over the years.

There I was again—lonely and even more damaged and in mourning—just like I was when I was eighteen. This time I was mourning me, the person I was convinced I could never become. I was mourning the life I knew I never could have, the mother I would never have, the family, the friends, and the father I'd never know. I was mourning it all. I just woke up and accepted my circumstances as my life. I was certain that my sole purpose in life was to be miserable. I told myself that I was needed so the world could have its balance. Some people are meant to have good lives and others are put here to suffer. That's right, to me there were the "good lives" and there were the "sufferers." I came up with this theory all on my own. I accepted my destiny.

It was about this time in my life when, if I ever had any morals, I certainly no longer retained them. I had no respect for myself or others. I didn't care. I didn't care about life or anything in it or about it. I figured there was no longer a point in trying to be a "good person." My life was going to always be what it was for it's not my fate to be happy, not ever. I had no values, no self-respect, no dignity. I didn't care about anything.

I'd grow to learn the hard way that some relationships are circumstantial, and some friendships are too.

Yvonne Gurley

15 Roller Coasters

I appeared to always look busy. I looked busy at home so when Byron or his family was there they couldn't talk to me. I was even too busy for my own family as they could barely get a call through. I was busy for everybody. I didn't want to know no one's business and I didn't want anyone to know mine, so I was busy minding my business!

I can see how I would seem somewhat mysterious to those at work. As I stated, no one could get a conversation in but Jamaica. I had really shut down because Byron had found himself in jail—again! To be honest, I was kind of relieved he was in jail because this meant I would take myself to work and not let him drop me off only to be extremely late picking me up or not bother to pick me up all; yea that was still going on, too. Like I stated I was still stupid. I'll say it for you, I hadn't learned a thing.

There were plenty of attractive guys at work; however, the last thing I wanted was another human in my face. It didn't stop them though. I was engaged but who could tell. Byron would pawn my ring so much I hardly wore the thing. We had no honor or respect for our engagement and, well, nobody did. Now to me, I didn't look like much. I felt like I had totally let myself go. Over the years, Byron had convinced me that no one would ever love me or want to be with me but him, with my issues and all. I had managed to lose my baby weight and I had slimmed all the way down thanks to my pill addiction since I was barely eating. To me, I was just this short, skinny, brown-skinned girl with no life or light inside her. I felt the best thing, well, the only thing I had going for my appearance was my hair. I always had a nice head of hair. With my sister being a beautician, despite everything, she made sure my hair was always presentable. I wore it simple, always just down or in a ponytail, as my hair stopped at the middle of my back. Other than that, again to me, I didn't look like much. I didn't find myself attractive in those days. I didn't believe I was pretty since I was in high school and even then, I think I was lying to myself.

My self-esteem had always been low because I always thought people could see my scars no matter how much I tried to hide them. No matter how many boyfriends I had in school, it never made me feel any better about myself. I was never single in all my years of school and as soon as I graduated, in walked Byron. Not only was I never single, but I also tended to date the popular guys. Still, I would drill the guys I dated about what they saw in me, in hopes of them somehow convincing me to love myself. I thought if I learned why they always claimed to love me, I might be able to love myself for the same reasons. Obviously, that never worked. No one can teach you how to love yourself or give you the reasons why. I don't care how many books you read or sermons you listen to, that is a journey that only you and God can take. He is the only one who can truly show you what love is and how to love

yourself or anyone else for that matter. Sadly enough, I was about to leave that responsibility all up to the next person who hopped on my rollercoaster of a life. I didn't just leave love up to this person; I left everything up to this person. I would put my values, morals, and selfworth all into the hands of a human being.

I never flew to London—London came to me. Unfortunately, I let him in with no passport, no two hundred dollars to pass, nothing. I broke all the rules and I let him in. It happened so fast I didn't even see it coming or take time to think about it. Those days I wasn't thinking much about anything I did; I was just doing, just being. I didn't have an identity. As I mentioned, I was doing the bare minimum it took to be considered alive.

Everyone loved them some London. The guys wanted to be London and the women wanted to be with London. At every office there is a London, I don't care where you work. He was popular inside and outside the office. The women were drooling over him, no matter their race. Everybody was throwing themselves at him. Guys envied him because London had this look about him that exuded confidence and fearlessness, one wouldn't dare go at him at all. He did not play that way though he never had to say it—you just knew. He had perfect teeth and the whitest, brightest smile. London had dark skin and the body of a Greek or Roman soldier. He was six-foot-two with dark wavy hair popping but a business-in-the-front, party-in-the-back type of thing with his ducktail growing in the back. Nonetheless, the homeboy was still fine, fine to everyone but me. I personally couldn't see what all the fuss was about because I really was all in my own head, still very much busy minding my business when he approached.

He was smooth at first, being very passive. He would only speak to me and keep pushing until his rattling on would turn into small talk. His one sentences grew into three to five sentences. Then he began to tell me jokes. I'm actually pretty goofy and, despite my circumstances, I never lost my sense of humor. It didn't take much to make me laugh; all a person had to do was try. No one had tried to make me smile in years so his persona threw me off. The small talks and jokes kept me off my busy as a bee game.

When a position became available in the medical coding department, I jumped on the chance to finally be working in the field for which I had studied. I landed the position and transferred to a different department. Byron was out of jail and back to his routine of dropping me off at work and not picking me up at all or extremely late. I was back in a training class for my new department. It was a proud moment for me, though my life with Byron would never allow happiness to reach its fullest potential. Anyway, the training class I was in was much smaller than my last one and everyone really began to get to know each other—not my cup of tea at all. One lady, in particular, began to take notice of Byron dropping me off and picking me up late and witnessing me calling for another ride home on several occasions, though I never noticed. Oh yes, she was noisy. At first, I didn't appreciate it but looking back, her noisiness probably saved my life.

Her name was Ms. Dee. Apparently, she and another Caucasian woman had been discussing my transportation issues. Since we were in training and on the same schedule, we ate lunch together. On our lunch breaks, they would start telling me about their lives and things they had gone through. All my life I was under the impression that white people didn't have issues. I just never met anyone Caucasian with a hard life. All the problems I ever witnessed from them usually just stemmed from being spoiled and not getting their way about something.

The women shared their stories with me. Ms. Dee told me all about her marriage with her first husband. She told me how she needed surgery on her knee for in her younger years she actually shot herself in the knee in an attempt to shoot her husband. She told me about how miserable she was being married to him and the abuse she suffered. As time went on, once she felt I was comfortable with her, she advised me to leave Byron! She said, "Now I don't know everything, in fact, I'm sure I don't know much at all about what you have going on, but what I do know is you are being mistreated." Here

again, someone was telling me I was bleeding. I tried to play stupid but she had caught me red-handed. She went on to say, "I see the way he drops you off and doesn't pick you up. I've heard you on a phone call or two finding another way
home. It isn't right, you know."

The other lady who had been sharing her life too decided it was a good time for her to chime in as well. That was when I realized it was an intervention! There was no escape as I had to go to work and get through training. I was so upset that I complained to Jamaica about it; she believed it was my fault they discovered any part of my business, as she and I were discreet about our personal lives. Bless her heart, Ms. Dee worked on me every chance she got to convince me that I deserved better, that I was stronger than I thought, and that I was covered by God. Little did she know I hadn't spoken to God since I was a teen. I was angry at first at the ladies but I'm so glad they didn't just talk about me behind my back but rather they stepped in. They shared their thoughts and it changed my life forever. Their bravery made me brave and bold, but in the wrong way at first.

London was still managing to tell me his jokes on occasion whenever we ran into each other in the breakroom or hallway. Between our small talk and the women in training, my rollercoaster stopped being so scary. I was still on the ride but it started to actually become a thrill like it was always meant to be. It had stopped for a long pause to allow London, my new job position, and a few others on, but then it started heading up again. I had no clue what would be on the other side as we climbed.

"Now, I don't know everything, in fact, I'm sure I don't know much at all about what you have going on, but what I do know is you are being mistreated."

16 High

Before I go any further, I know Stacey's actions may have made you feel some type of way. Maybe some of her choices might have offended you thus far. It certainly offended young adult Stacey. Maybe you've never been alone in a room with somebody you had no business being left alone with but if I might refresh your memory Stacey's life began with her being left alone in rooms with people, she had no business being with. Some of you may be judging because by the grace of God you made all the right decisions, somebody had the decency to pray for you and there are no skeletons to be found in your closet. Yeah you never dated anybody's boyfriend or husband according to what he said or perhaps you just never found out that you did. Sure, everyone you ever dated was single, celibate, and in waiting. What you thought was love has never left you baffled. What you thought was love never asked you to become somebody or do some things that would one day bring you shame or embarrassment if anybody ever found out. Life has never disappointed you, brought you so much pain, or filled you with so much fear that everyday your only wish is to not wake up. If and when you get to sleep "wherever I end up when I finally close my eyes Lord, I'm praying it's better than this place right here," is what I would whisper in my soul. You were never young; you were never unwise, not mature. Possibly you're thinking in no way, shape, or form, was young Stacey ever you! Did my coworkers see parts of themselves in me, or was it pure empathy? No matter what it was they exemplified grace and partnered it with mercy.

I guess I just needed somebody to say it, someone, to say something. That little intervention had my mind spinning more than usual. I had been abused my whole life and it seemed as though no one ever noticed but me — so much so that even I stopped noticing.

After all, Byron had done to me, why didn't I demand my money back from him when he received his tattle tale money? Why didn't I make him pay? Why didn't I just do something, anything? I guess it's the same reasons my abusers never paid for their actions. Why were they never punished? Why was nothing ever done and why was I given nothing?

There were Byron's many addictions, not to mention all of the other women he would later confess he was sleeping with, including one of my best friends, though I never told either of them I knew. All I did was numb myself into Dumbville by taking those anti-depressants. So, I'm forced to ask myself: was I stupid, high, or both? After a certain point, even if I tried to claim ignorance and being duped; he proved himself worthy of leaving time after time yet I stayed. Why did I stay? I stayed because the child in me believed there was nothing I could do about it. I accepted my conditions as my life; suffering had always been my life.

After a while, I can't keep pointing the finger at Byron for doing this and that. I have to admit that by continuing to stay; I was abusing myself and getting high. It's a hard truth to face but it took me several more years and mistakes to truly break free because I chose to get high and numb myself. I chose to do what everyone around me did—I silenced the truth. Stacey, I couldn't do better by you, because nobody did better by me.

I used to think my triggers for my panic attacks were just my past showing up to torture me; however, those triggers were just guards, dancing around the truth. Triggers are merely our deepest truths dangling around the keys to which would set us free! Like I stated, the truth was always visiting me, always wanting me to be free. Only, I couldn't see the truth as keys to my freedom from everything.

When I was younger, I said never to a lot of things, we all did. I bet most of you are somewhere or done something you said you'd never do, somewhere you claimed you'd never be. Forgive yourself for it. I know I had to; I still do. Back then, I was eating all the "never" I had claimed. Little did I know I was about to be eating even more.

> Never say Never
>
> Down through there
>
> Is where you've taken me
>
> I'm emotional, upset, I'm angry
>
> Down through there
>
> Is where I said I would never go
>
> But oh, lo and behold
>
> How I just didn't know
> I underestimated
>
> The power of love and affection
>
> No one ever told me
>
> That loving someone requires protection
>
> "Go in with an open heart"
>
> Well, do you know what I say to that?
>
> Pack your bags honey
>
> Cause you're about to be taken for a ride And
>
> you are never coming back!
>
> Down through there
>
> Is where I said I would never go "Never
>
> say Never" huh?
>
> Now I know

Ms. Dee sparked something in me. She got me thinking I actually had a chance at life. She also sparked something else. Byron had really been on his worse behavior at that point as if it could get any worse. Online bill pay wasn't quite an option for bills at that time and I really needed him to pay the bills while I was at work. You already know what I'm about to tell you—he was back to his old ways of not paying bills. I'd come home from work or he'd call me and I'd have to find out the water was turned off or the cable, or the internet; no matter what it was something was always getting turned off even though I had already given him the money to pay the bills.

While we're on the subject, let me just point out that I worked for a top insurance company as well as a pharmacy yet I was using a government-issued cell phone because I couldn't for the life of me keep the phone on. Jamaica had banned me from using my little flip phone around her. Anytime I'd try to pull it out she'd say, "Girl, put that thing up. Here take my phone." Sometimes I'd have to use Facebook to talk to anyone due to my lack of a working cell phone. I was one of those people who always had a new phone number.

It wasn't just the phone; I finally concluded I would never have anything if I remained with Byron. Every day I stayed I felt a little bit of my life being sucked out of me. Really, I did. My life with him took such a toll on my body it was actually breaking down. I was sick all the time. It began to be just like it was when I was a kid. Ultimately,

I ended up with a benign tumor in the back of my head that was surgically removed. After the tumor, I told myself if I didn't leave, I wasn't going to survive this life or this relationship with Byron too much longer. He was continuing to steal, lie, and cheat. I was continuing to numb myself, which was no longer enough.

Earlier, I asked myself was I stupid, high, or both. The answer was I didn't care. It was never that I couldn't see what Byron was doing or that I didn't have enough sense to leave. It's not even just about being high. Somewhere, at some point, I stopped caring about me. Looking back, I wonder if I ever truly cared about me at all because if I did I would have never ended up with Byron in the first place.

I used to think it was Byron that turned me into damaged goods but truth be told I was damaged goods when he got me, he just made it worse. Some part of me had to have already given up to even entertain Byron at all. It wasn't Byron that started my journey of not loving myself—I didn't love myself from the start.

There was a lingering sense of guilt for my mental and emotional state. How could I properly love my daughter if I didn't even know how to properly love myself or even know the true definition of love. I felt bad for not being a "happy mom." I felt bad about everything. The amount of guilt I felt about Byron being her father period could have its own section of remorse.

Triggers are merely our deepest truths dangling around the keys to which would set us free!

Yvonne Gurley

17 Control

After I recovered from surgery, I began to have thoughts, all kinds of thoughts. I was having you or me type of thoughts. I wanted Byron to pay. I wanted him to feel just an ounce of what I had been feeling for so many years. All the women, the drugs, the money, stealing, lying, sex, and porn addiction—I had enough of it all!

I refused to take any accountability, as this was all his fault. I needed him to see what he had done to me, what he was doing to me. I realized later God needed me to see what I was doing to myself but it would be a long time before I'd get to that conclusion. You see, when God gave us free will he didn't add the word "sometimes." I can't blame God for other peoples' actions and I can't blame him for my own.

Ms. Dee's story about her attempt to shoot her husband really sparked the wrong plug. This man's family allowed this woman to marry a man they knew was schizophrenic and nobody told her. For years this woman suffered alone. Nobody have a sit down with you about how to be with a schizophrenic person? How in the world was she supposed to be equipped for that? Just like no one had any sit downs with me about how to be with someone who had all of Byron's addictions. I felt like I was running out of options, if I ever had any. I knew physically harming him wasn't the answer so I went to see a therapist because my pills could no longer calm these thoughts in my head. I needed someone else to take control. I was afraid of what I might do had I held on to control any longer.

My initial reason for seeing a therapist was for the sole purpose of getting switched to a better drug but God had other plans. It was a requirement to talk to the doctor in order to get the pills. The doctor who prescribed the pills couldn't take on any more patients at the time, so I got stuck with a therapist who not only didn't prescribe medicine but she also didn't truly believe in taking pills at all. I was stuck with a Christian doctor (Yep, Jesus play way too much)! Looking back, I can laugh about it now but it wasn't funny to me then.

Ah yes, the wonderful Dr. Yolla and I would spend many years unravelling my past. There were many hurdles along the way, as my present circumstances needed immediate attention. Therapy started out as being a pleasant distraction; however, there was one tiny, little problem—I started talking, which meant I started feeling, something I wasn't used to. The result was I panicked. As you can imagine, my sober living with this new therapist did not last long because she was making me feel stuff.

Knowing my therapist couldn't give me any meds, I turned to the clinic that originally prescribed my medication. Unfortunately, the medicine the doctor prescribed was way too expensive. Still, I had a good relationship with the clinic doctor and she found a way around the cost. The office received loads of drug samples so every time a new box of samples came in, the nurse would call me to schedule an appointment. The middleman had been cut

out—no therapy and no pharmacy. It was the ideal situation as the doctor and I were both getting exactly what we wanted. Don't be surprised, the medical field is not exempt from scandal. I used to think to myself as I popped another antidepressant, "Who wants to feel stuff?" I was back to the same old me, numb and not caring about anything; my singular goal in life was not to feel.

My new pills had numbed me so well that I even made the decision to continue to fight to keep my daughter in a home where she'd be raised by both parents, no matter how dysfunctional we were. I did it, I mean I actually set a day in which we were going to go down to the courthouse and apply for a marriage license. I even scheduled a date to have my IUD (a form a birth control) to be removed so we could have another child. Yea, I was high as high could be on those pills.

Work was still an escape for me. I was done with my training for my new department but Ms. Dee and I continued to chat from time to time. She'd ask me how everything was going because I appeared to be so much happier. What she did not realize was she was just seeing the glow from the pills. I wasn't a bit happier, though the pills even fooled me into thinking I was happier too.

Anyway, London and I would still randomly bump into each other from time to time and he'd still tell me his jokes. One morning I arrived to work and as soon as I opened my email, I had a message from him. At this time, I can't recollect all the email said and I certainly don't want to lie, as I have done enough of that. I'll just say the email let it be known there was something he had felt on his end between us. Being intrigued by this, I agreed. I mean, we did always somehow seem to be wondering the halls of the building or breakroom at the same time; that couldn't be just a coincidence, right? We must have emailed back and forth that entire day. For a moment I completely forgot about my date at the courthouse arriving soon. I forgot about everything.

When I had got home from work that evening I was paid a visit by Byron's mother. I know it seems as though she didn't like me, but that wasn't it at all. She was just highly misinformed of my character, which made it harder for her to like or understand me. This is what I told myself about anyone who didn't like me. At times, we actually had really good talks. Anyway, on that particular day I was walking her out as we were finishing our conversation in the driveway when Byron pulled up in an unknown car. She quickly asked him what was going on and whose car was he driving. He carelessly stated it was his coworker Charity's car that she had loaned to him while he went on his break. I immediately walked back into the house and didn't say a word. His mother left in a state of confusion as she wanted to believe her son was a good person. I was kind of glad he made this screw up in front of her as I never had any proof of his disrespect. When Byron got home from work, I confronted him about the matter and his reply was "I didn't know I couldn't do that." This was his explanation for driving and coming home in another woman's car. I put his response in my back pocket and went off to bed.

    London and I continued to chat more and more about a little bit of everything, but never saw each other outside of work. One day I had to leave work early to stop by Byron's job. When I went inside the retail store he worked, I couldn't find him, even his coworkers didn't know where he was. I passed by the breakroom and I had saw Charity in the room smiling as she was talking to someone I couldn't see. I waited as I tried to get her attention but once she saw me through the breakroom window, it was as if she saw a ghost—her white face quickly got even whiter. She hurriedly burst through the doors silent as the night. Normally, she would speak to me, as all his coworkers were friendly with me. Nonetheless, I knew the moment I saw Charity's reaction who she was talking to and exactly what was going on. After she stormed out of the breakroom, Byron calmly followed with this big, stupid smile on his face in an effort to "play it cool." I looked at him with disgust and just left as his coworkers witnessed the entire thing. I was so embarrassed as they too had caught on to what was going on though they both had been denying their involvement.

Have you ever been so tired and so frustrated with your life as a whole that you just wanted to hand it over to somebody else and say, "Here, you do it!"

You see, when God gave us free will he didn't add the word "sometimes." I can't blame God for other peoples' actions and I can't blame him for my own.

18 Fears

The warning label said
This man could leave you dead
Heartbroken
Or all outside your head
So, don't take
Too much of his love
It's not good stuff
He'll make you cry
He'll tear you up
With his goodbyes
That's what the warning label said
That's what the warning label said…

 I wrote the song "Warning Labels" about this time. I was feeling so many emotions, emotions I never felt before. I felt things I didn't know existed to feel. I just wished some people, some things, came with warning labels. I began to dive deeper into conversations with

London. I remember one day handing him something at work and the tip of my fingers must have touched his and I felt this surge of energy. I know you're thinking it was a regular, innocent, and mildly touch but it was a shock, like some sort of static, but no, I felt real energy pass between us. It freaked me out. I was going to keep it to myself but as soon as I got back to my desk London had already emailed me asking if I had felt that charge of energy that shifted through. I was intrigued that he was open-minded enough to not deny an actual experience for fear of being weird. We would ponder on what that was for our entire relationship.

London had come to the realization that I was floating and wanted to know what I was floating on. I told him and he curiously tried one of my pills. It was hilarious when he started itching the entire day. He had his own choice of vices to keep himself numb too. I knew why I wanted to be numb but I didn't know why he did.

He always appeared to be so happy, always seem to have it all together. One day I must have really looked at him in such a way that I saw behind that perfect smile was an imperfect soul. I saw the pain behind his eyes that day and I wanted to know what caused it. I asked him about it but at first he wouldn't budge until we eventually found ourselves peering into each other's souls all the time. We used to never talk or have any interaction outside of work but later we began to find that we missed each other's conversation after work so we finally started to speak beyond emails. After all these years, I finally resolved my phone situation. At the time, my conversations with London was one of my few sources of happiness and I wasn't about to let Byron ruin it. I felt like Norbit.

One night, I went to sleep like I always did after taking my pills and, as usual, Byron was not at home. This was

Nobody's Baby

our norm so I thought nothing of it until Byron woke me up in a rage. He had gone through my phone and saw my conversations with London. I tried to just leave the room but he cornered me, yelling and screaming at the top of his lungs. When he asked me about our dealings, I quickly responded, "Oh, I didn't know I couldn't do that. Now are you done because I have to be at work in the morning and I would like to get some sleep?" That infuriated him even more. Byron began punching the wall right by my face to intimidate me. My two-and-a-half-year-old daughter witnessed it all.

Because I had been through so much physical abuse in my childhood, it took quite a bit to even make me flinch. When Byron saw I had no fear in my eyes, his began to fill with it because he didn't know what I was going to do next. After he finished destroying the wall with his fist, I again asked him if he was done and he moved out of my way as I proceeded to bed. My daughter was so confused by the whole situation. She began to yell at him and tell him, "Daddy you better clean that up," pointing to the plaster all over the floor. Knowing my daughter was distraught by this, I decided I had to do something. Seeing my daughter so unhappy did something to my spirit. My own unhappiness never ignited anything in me but my daughters did. I know this sounds strange, but I'm glad I witnessed her so unhappy. I say this because if there's one thing Stacey would learn is that happiness does not inspire change. It is the discomfort, the frustration, thoughts of "I have to do something" that truly makes us thrive.

The next day, I had already made up my mind to leave. There was no way I could stay. We were too far gone years ago but I was just accepting it. The pills couldn't numb this realization away. That morning when I got to work, I told London all about it in which he was very disturbed. I told him how unhappy I was as I had never given him the impression that I wasn't. For all he knew, I was just this engaged chick who was willing to cheat on her soon-to-be husband. That husband thing was not going to happen, at least not with Byron anyway.

I proceeded to ask London about his love life since I had opened up to him so much. He stated he was actually happy and there were no problems on his end as far as relationships were considered. I was confused, and thought he had to be lying because he was doing everything I was doing and anybody, male or female, so dang, 'happy' wouldn't be doing that. I brushed it under the rug and told myself he'd eventually open up about it.

Then Jamaica had told me she saw in the paper that he had gotten married. I quickly asked him about it, which seemed to upset him. He didn't realize that when you applied for a marriage license they published it in the newspaper. When I asked him if he indeed did get married he denied it and gave the notion that the license was only applied, not processed. I actually believed him. Who was I to judge considering I was about to be in that same predicament, had I actually made it to the courthouse. I knew plenty of people who applied for the license yet never got married so I never bothered to ask him about it again.

Nobody's Baby

On one of the last days living with Byron, he and I began to argue, though I can't remember what about. I do recall I wanted to get away from him, as there was no need to argue in my opinion. But he wouldn't shut up so I grabbed my pills and ran to the bathroom. He proceeded to bang on the door and yell but I remained silent. I just sat on the bathroom floor wishing I could be anywhere but in that moment. I refused to say a word to him. He began to punch holes right through the bathroom door until he could see me clearly. I thought to myself, "Oh he really lost his mind now!" It was at that point he exclaimed, "I thought you were trying to kill yourself, man. I didn't know what you were doing." My response was simple and true: "Over you? Ain't nobody 'bout to commit no suicide over you. I wouldn't give you the pleasure of having that story to tell." The nerve!

Finally, I mustered up the strength to leave Byron after seven years. After all those years of misery with him, I took my daughter and we left. Though I was strongly against therapy at first; desperation required me to try all alternate routes. My resistance to therapy built the necessary muscle. I have to admit that my sessions with Dr. Yolla actually convinced me that I could do it. "If everything you've mentioned about your life is true, then everything you feel and everything you don't want to feel are more than valid. You need time, space to sort through those feelings and that can never happen in the circumstances that you're in with Byron." London convinced me, too. The thing was though I left Byron in fear. I had been with him since I was eighteen and I was turning twenty-five. Since I know better now, when I look back at young Stacey I could see that I was still that eighteen-year-old girl when I left. I spent almost that entire relationship numbing myself, not learning from any of my experiences, not maturing in any way. I was just as ignorant when I left Byron as I was when I got with him. I was just as blind and just as broken, if not even more broken than before. I knew nothing about being single and dating, as I had always had a boyfriend since I was old enough to have one. I don't know why young Stacey was so afraid.

Technically, I had been single that entire seven years since Byron did not really participate in the relationship. I thought I didn't know how to be a single mother when in fact I had always been a single mother. Byron never shared in the care of our daughter. Also, I always paid all of the bills so really, the only difference was the location. I was actually going to be living completely separate form Byron and his misery.

Happiness does not inspire change. It is the discomfort, the frustration, the thoughts of "I have to do something" that truly makes us thrive.

19 Impulse

When you're afraid or find yourself in a situation in which you deem scary, often times you act on impulse. You don't think or see things clearly; you just do! Whatever you end up doing may not always be what was best for you. In fact, what you do may not be you at all. I believe that was exactly the case for me and London.

Who I was at the time I couldn't tell you. My entire identity was wrapped up in my connection to Byron. I didn't know who I was apart from him and his family. Finding this out was more than scary for me. I never tried to explore my identity before and now I was being forced to start that journey. I began to dig even deeper in therapy after an incident with London I didn't care to explain happened. You see London knew all about the depths of my unhappiness with Byron but he still didn't know me. Even Jamaica, whom I proclaimed to tell everything to, didn't know me as I only told her about my unhappiness with Byron because that was what was obvious. I never allowed her to know me—the real me. I didn't allow anybody, not even myself or God, or so I thought.

After staying with friends for a few weeks, I monstered up the money to get my own two-bedroom apartment for my daughter and me. My mother gave me zero support throughout this process and I was infuriated with her because once again she reminded me that I was motherless. She was always reminding me I was "nobody's baby." To me, she was just the woman who gave birth and nothing more. She let it be known that she did not approve of me leaving Byron, as she believed in staying together no matter what (another lesson my mother taught me). She didn't know the full details of my misery with him over the years and didn't care to know.

One night, London was over and attempted to hold me as I slept. I'm not sure as to what happened or what I did or said to him, as I just know the next morning he proceeded to tell me he believes I had been "touched" as a child and he wanted to talk about it. Byron mentioned something of this nature in previous years but I brushed it off when I realized he didn't truly care about the severity of my childhood pain as he, like my family, felt I was lying and nothing ever happened to me at all since I was just crazy. He stated this after I had accused him of drug use. I was used to Stacey's truths always being turned into Stacey's outlandish lies.

London was different from Byron in so many ways, but in this situation, he really wanted to know what happened to me. He drilled me for months. I had therapy with Dr. Yolla *and* with London. The more I talked, the more I felt and expressed to both of them my reoccurring nightmare from my past. There was an incident between my mother and I of which to this day she claims she does not remember.

    I was twelve-years old and I had asked her if I could go to the skating rink and for some reason this angered her. She told me no and I accepted the response and went to my room. Before I knew it, she had knocked me to the ground and proceeded to kick me over and over and over again. The skin of my legs began to rip, as she had on her sneakers. I thought the kicking would never end. The only thing that saved me was the asthma attack she had as she was pummeling me with her foot. She began to become short of breath and was forced to stop to get her inhaler. After mumbling some profanity, she left the room. I laid there on the floor helplessly, not even remembering crawling into bed. My sister had come home later that night and saw my condition; when I told her what had happened, she was outraged. She questioned our mother about it and my mother slapped her for her boldness. My sister left the house and did not return for a couple of days and I was alone in pain, as usual.

This night was on repeat when I tried to sleep. Other nights, more painful memories played in my head like someone created a playlist of the worst nights of Stacey's life and decided to play them when I went to bed. Dr. Yolla worked with me to learn how to conquer such nightmares, but I was a coward. I wanted to numb myself even in my sleep so I started taking a different set of pills at night to help drown out my unconscious thoughts when I slept.

As time progressed London and I grew closer. We couldn't stand the idea of being apart at any time we didn't have to. The nights we slept separately were far and in between. London would bear hug me in my sleep so I would no longer fight him. He did this until I got used to him being beside me. Byron would always just put a pillow between us or not sleep beside me all together. I wasn't accustomed to such efforts being made for me. I don't think I had ever been so vulnerable with anyone else until London came along. I told him everything. He knew every inch of me. He witnessed my deepest truths about my painful past that no one knew. Most women love the idea of being held by a man as they slept but for me my mind would tell me I was being held down against my will and something awful was about to happen. Being held or spooning felt like abuse and some days, even presently it still does.

Once he saw how vulnerable I was willing to be with him, he too became just as vulnerable. I had been right— that was indeed pain I saw behind those eyes. He began to divulge all his secrets and deepest truths. He expressed the pain that plagued him. He was numbing his feelings and past too, though he would never admit to it. I have decided not to share London's story as I don't feel it belongs to me to share. Due to this choice, it makes it quite difficult to talk about our relationship; without London's story I'm aware it would make it hard for one to truly understand him or the psychology behind our relationship but I feel it is for the best. The only thing I'm willing to share is that London knew exactly what it meant and how it felt to be "nobody's baby." It was a reality for him too and we indulged in our feelings about this quite often.

We were both going through major transitions in our lives and, whether we wanted to admit it or not, we were both afraid. We never actually expressed our fears to each other but we were anxious. No matter how old one becomes there are certain life circumstances in which you feel the need for parental guidance or wisdom. A simple "You can do this" or "It's going to be okay" would have been encouraging and we both needed that so dearly at that time. It's one thing to mourn a parent that is deceased but it's a whole other thing when a parent is alive. Every time you encounter or think about this parent, you have to let the parent you want them to be die a little every single time. If it sounds depressing that's because it is. This was something London and I both had to do.

There was something about London, me, and our relationship that somehow filled that hole inside that had always been there. I thought a hole was being filled, anyway. When you don't know what love is, it's difficult to know when you're truly getting it or not or if you're really being filled by love at all. Being with him made being "nobody's baby" a little bit easier, as it didn't hurt as much. Somehow I finally had my father figure. It was the same way for him as something in me reflected a mother and we were dangerously attached to each other. This was not a boyfriend and girlfriend thing, that would be too simple. We were way more complicated than that. We had a soul tie and an ungodly one at that. We knew our relationship was unhealthy and that we indeed were hurting not just ourselves but the people around us, but we just couldn't seem to let go. If you've ever experienced a soul tie, you know that I'm not making this up. You really can't just let go! Losing London would be like losing my father all over again and the same could be said for London with his mother. We wanted to fix in each other what we thought made our parents leave. Over time, we became closer than I had ever been with anyone.

As you can imagine, the day I found out he indeed was married I was devastated. We were both cheating, why on

Earth did he feel the need to lie? It made no sense. I get that I did end up leaving Byron, but still, why lie about it? We had gotten into an argument and his way of winning was screaming, "That's why I'm married." My whole world came crashing down on me. He practically lived with me. He never missed a phone call or text. He was always home in time for dinner and to tuck my daughter in for bed. We were almost always together. I never felt like we were in hiding or I was a secret at all. I couldn't wrap my mind around how he was able to pull this off. I eventually found out his girlfriend had moved to another state and had been waiting for him to ultimately move there with her.

Considering we talked about marriage and kids, even taking a family photo, how could I fathom he was on his way to getting married or already fully married? He spent so much time with me, how could I? He had been around my entire family and I had met plenty of his as well. I felt betrayed in a way I didn't even know existed. We had shared so much together. After his truth came about, he revealed his ideas of polygamy. This was his logical explanation for pursuing me.

Now that I know better, the truth was always there dangling its keys in front of me; I just refused to grasp them. I cannot blame him or anybody. I cannot be angry because in the depths of all of us the truth indeed is really always there. The reality is we just don't want to face it. It was the beginning of the end of us, we didn't want to face the truth; we would go back and forth for what seemed like forever, both of us slowly letting go but not really wanting to. So now I had yet another person that I had to mourn, and so did he. I got over London lying to me simply because it wasn't a pain I had never felt. Honestly, I hurt him just as much in other ways because that's what broken people do.

We tried to coach one another through that grieving process but that was unsuccessful. We only ended up hurting each other even more as time progressed. To this day, it's still a very fragile subject to me. I know it would be quite entertaining to go into all the depths of us but I cannot. It would be too painful. We were never about your average physical attraction; we connected on pain and our opinions about life, nothing else.

London understood me so much because he was always right there with me. Whenever I felt a way, he had just recovered from feeling that way, and vice versa. I was secretly what society would consider the "awkward black girl" and he was secretly the "awkward black guy," yet no one knew this but us.

"You go through cycles and moments in life. All I can say is take advantage of the energy. If you're feeling like learning and educating and being isolated take advantage. Deep thoughts, isolation, and just general confusion are very normal and necessary. Do self-reflection and determine your direction and just focus. Being still is as important as going. Being alone is as necessary as having friends. Not having direction is as important as knowing where you're going. Find your balance and just always know you are ok no matter what,

Yours truly, London!"

20 Denial

Are you disappointed? Well, I was too! You may want me to relive my relationship with London but I apologize in advance for I cannot. You see, that hurt me to the deepest core that one could be hurt. Losing London was worse than my childhood and my relationship with Byron because London *knew* me.

> When we lied
> Our souls tied
> Leaving us forever connected
> Forever imbedded
> He would be with me
> And from then on
> I reaped
> Of the demons he keeps
> From then on, he would be
> Trapped in my mind
> Forever inside of me
> Obsessed with everything about him

Nobody's Baby

    Thoughts of him over a thousand times

    Thoughts of everything we once were

Replaying over and over again

Inside my mind

Because after a while

That same person he was no longer

See I loved that first person

And so forever I hungered

To lie with him again

Most of all I missed my best friend

See I thought our troubled souls

Was a blessing but it has been

More of a curse

All that we had in common

Only makes things worse

It only makes it hurt

See that's what happens when

Your pain is understood

Use understanding against me

He would,

Torture my already tortured soul

Re-breaking what he healed

Never allowing me to be whole

Forcing me to feel

Everything that he ever felt

So, his pain with my pain
    Caused my heart to melt

    Not in a good way

    In all ways, that is bad

    Feelings of depression and anger

    Causing everything in me to go mad

    I almost lost everything in me

    I mean I almost lost my mind

    All because of a place

    I wanted to remain in time

    Because when we lied

    Our souls tied

    Leaving me breathless

    And I felt less of me And more

    of him

    Remember how I asked if you'd ever been so frustrated that you'd just hand your life to someone to do it for you? Well, that's what I did. I handed all of my hurt and all of my pain over to London. I put everything in his hands. I made him responsible for my happiness and my healing. Over time, he had convinced me that he could save me and protect me from everything and I foolishly believed him. To me, London was Superman! Being a "nobody's baby" is not about just having a boyfriend or girlfriend. If you thought that's what it meant you're mistaken. No loving relationship can cure this. No amount of physical attraction would ever do. This was about someone getting to know you, really know you from inside and out. The type of love that knows exactly how you got every scar you have on your body and not just the ones on the outside but the ones you have on the inside, too. This wasn't the love in which you can finish each other's sentences; it was the love that knows what you're about to say before you even think to say it. It was a love that could feel something was wrong before a sign was ever shown. I couldn't possibly make this up. I know I'm a writer and all but there are some things even the wildest imagination cannot imagine. Some things can only be described simply because you felt it, because you lived it, because it was once something you called yours.

    I know for you it would be quite entertaining for me to tell you about the night I stood at my doorstep crying as he was leaving because our time was up. You want to know about how I fell to the floor literally in physical pain because the agony that shot through my body when he left was more than my soul could bare. Before I go any further, I want to make clear that this pain was not onesided. I was hurting but it wasn't just me. *We* were hurting.

    Deep down inside I knew I would never have what London and I had again and to this day I haven't and I don't want to. The amount of pressure we put on one another was unrealistic. I feel like I made him my god. Young Stacey thought to herself, who's love could ever compare to mine and London's. I didn't think anyone could top it. I told myself I'd never open up to anyone like that again, I'll never be so vulnerable. Though I had stopped writing while I was with Byron, I wrote song after song, poem after poem while with London. He wrote as well. We sparked something in each other. We both concluded that we fully understood what it meant to have a muse and found it funny, but only when it wasn't hurting. While I was dealing with the hurt of London I was also dealing with Byron and the drama that came with the aftermath of leaving him. Yes, honey that plague was still alive and well in my life even though I was long gone. The house on Sunnydale wasn't feeling so sunny for Byron now that he was alone. Maybe to him it once was but for me it never did.

To distract myself, I started working out at the gym. I had put on quite a few pounds with London and now had a small pouch. London and I loved to eat, or maybe it was our love for food plus the munchies, who knows! Anyway, my paternal cousin had reached out and asked if I'd work out with her at the gym. I was such a people pleaser at the time I said yes to almost everything in my twenties. After our first workout though, I quickly decided the gym was my new favorite place. I enjoyed working out but I also enjoyed seeing all the men working out. Now before you judge me, need I remind you I had been stuck with Byron for seven years and I was so heartbroken over London. I'm just saying! Have a little mercy for Stacey. The mature version of me knows this was the worse place to be after a breakup since there were options everywhere. I couldn't wait to get off of work and go to the gym.

I'd spend all day at work listening to sad love songs. I used all of my breaks to run to my car so I could cry alone in peace. Every time I'd begin to lighten up on taking the pills, it seemed like some new heartache would come and I'd use it as an excuse to keep taking them. The gym was my only escape from everything I was feeling and everything I was thinking.

Nobody's Baby

You would think the last person I'd need to befriend at the gym was a male stripper but you guessed it. Yep, young Stacey really knew how to pick them! Naturally, he was popular. Everyone knew him and everyone wanted him and to be honest, almost everyone had him. Did I care about any of this—absolutely not! I just wanted to be distracted from my hurt feelings because the pills didn't always cut it.

London found out about this new friendship and become angry with me. No matter how much time would pass without communication, if he found out about something he didn't like he'd reach out to me and let me know exactly how he felt about my choices. In the long run, London would find out about everybody. For the longest time I couldn't put my finger on how he always knew where I was and if I was talking to someone new. He would send a random text and say, "Let's just say it's somebody that you think is your friend but isn't." Now, the last person I would have ever thought he was getting all his information from was Jamaica. She never talked to him directly, as she proclaimed to not like him, but what she was doing was far crueler. What that woman did and said to me I don't think any friend before she could have topped it. Get ready, this is so wrong y'all!

As it turns out, Jamaica was never really my friend. In fact, she never truly liked me at all. There was a woman at work, June, who was always on the lookout for others' business. I'll never understand what people got out of that, but she was one—and so was Jamaica, but I never knew. Anyway, Jamaica had only become friends with me to know my business so she and June could swap tales of their daily gossip. I was merely entertainment for them.

Jamaica would ask me what I was doing on the weekend or who I was dating and I'd blindly and honestly reply. She would report her news to June who would then report to London. June would never admit to being attracted to London, but for what other reason would someone be so involved in someone else's personal life? June also made it her business to tell management about my relationship with London but no one really cared. Nonetheless, for over a year Jamaica would make conversation with me and then report back her info; shortly after, London would become upset and treat me like he was psychic or something.

It took me years before I realized Jamaica was not my friend. The reason why I never suspected her was because she wasn't the only person June sent to get to know me. There was another woman at work who had befriended me as well; however, she grew to like me so much that she confessed. June had sent her to get to know me because she wanted to understand why I was attracting guys. You know how women can be! I was grateful Queen had admitted the truth to me but I couldn't trust her after that. Though she tried to prove herself as harmless, I could never allow myself to really be friends with her because of her initial reasoning for involving herself with me. I never would have suspected June had not one but two spies working on her behalf.

Back to the stripper! He had invited me to a show he was doing. I never went to see any strippers perform so my sister and I gathered up some friends and we all went. When I stepped one foot inside the party, I got a text from London telling me to look to my left. That crazy man was sitting there looking right at me. His little grapevine had let him in on everything. He proceeded to pull me outside where we fussed back and forth. For some strange reason, he felt I should stay with him and be faithful. Was he kidding me? After we reached a certain point, he hopped in his car and took off so I went right back inside, not worried about London or his threats.

I finished watching the show and left; I realized I didn't like strip shows, but I did like the excitement of hanging out with a stripper for some reason. He and I would chat from time to time. He knew all about London, as anyone I ever associated with knew about London because he made sure his existence was known no matter if my friend was male or female.

The stripper would always try to convince me to be healthy as I was always very open and honest about my pills. London never cared for my pill habit either but he had his own vices so I didn't think he should preach about mine. The stripper and I never got very close, as I knew better. I'd hang around with his crew and share some laughs and we'd all poke fun at each other. I remember one day going to the gym counter and he was pulling his money out to pay for something and I fell out laughing. I laughed because he had a bunch of one's as I automatically assumed, he got them from stripping. He had a regular job as well but the idea of him using his stripping money to pay for something was quite amusing to me. Him knowing my sense of humor by now instantly tried to defend himself and said, "See, now this not even from that." He couldn't tell me anything. I had already made it up in my mind that it was his stripping money and so did the rest of his friends when they realized why I was laughing so hard. We clowned him all night.

Speaking of nights, my stripper friend would randomly wake me up out of my sleep. One night when I answered the phone in a very sleepy voice he told me he was at my door. We had grabbed a bite to eat and road around the city after the gym a few times so he knew where I lived. I opened the door and let him in, asking what was going on because I was confused and sleepy. He pushed passed me and kept asking me, "Where they at? Where they at?" Being confused, I asked him what he was referring to and he replied, "The pills, your pills. Where they at? Where you keep them?" At that point I explained if he wanted some pills he just had to ask but he became angry and impatient and began going through my entire house looking for my stash. It just so happened my pills were under the bathroom cabinet in my bedroom. He pushed me out of the bathroom and locked the door. Mind you, it was two or three in the morning and my nighttime pills had me high, sleepy, and again, confused! When I got in the bathroom, he flushed all of my pills. I tried to jump on his back but I was no match for him. He had gotten rid of everything and I started yelling at him asking him what was wrong with him and why he did it. He yelled right back at me explaining he had an uncle who died from a pill addiction and he couldn't and wouldn't lose me like that. I just stared at him like a deer in headlights. I remember thinking, "Um, I didn't know I mattered." I had no words. I wasn't used to anyone caring about me but London and even he hadn't dared attack my pill habit.

After that incident, the stripper said his peace and we just sat there a while until I walked him out. It was one of the strangest moments I'd ever witnessed besides with London. The stripper and I never again talked about that night and he never brought my pills up to me again. He told me once that he knew I wanted him to save me but he couldn't because he wanted me to save myself even though I wouldn't. To be honest, I didn't know how.

I had been in such denial about so much that I wasn't even aware that I even had an addiction. I always thought because the antidepressants were prescribed instead of narcotics that I was different. I didn't think I had a drug problem. I was in complete denial about my pill usage and addiction. I was in denial about a lot of things actually. To this day, I never thanked the stripper for his heroic acts or told him how much that night and what he did meant to me. A lot of women have bashed him publicly over the years and have had a lot of negative things to say, but I am one who could never utter a bad word about him. Maybe others experienced something awful with him but my experience was something I always held dear.

We never turned into anything. I doubt he'd ever read this tale of mine but I want you, the reader, to know that after his act I never touched those pills again. Though I still experimented for a while, it was the beginning of my many efforts to walk away from my addiction. I have to admit it was because he showed me that somebody was paying attention and somebody cared. Sometimes, that's all you need in life.

I always thought because the antidepressants were prescribed, instead of being narcotics, that I was different. I didn't think I had a drug problem.

21 Unpacked

Dear father, I repent
For all the time I spent
Drowning in my sorrow
With no hopes for tomorrow

Perhaps hopelessness is not even a sin
But for me being hopeless
Is where my sin began

Thoughts of not being worthy
Frustrated because nobody chose me
Feeling like nobody loved me
Lead me down the wrong path
Poisoning myself as
Satan held his belly and laughed

All the while, I cried
Too numb to let the tears fall
So, I cried on the inside

Yvonne Gurley
Rehearsing all my pitfalls

Miserable, because I felt I was never chosen
Until the serpent said, "I'll choose you
But you have to let me swallow you whole then
Sit in my belly as I swallow you alive
I mean technically
You'll be alive but you'll be dead on the inside

On the inside of my tummy
It'll then be too late to start running
There is no point in screaming
Because you know nobody's coming
You're mine
Isn't being chosen what you wanted all this time?"

My life had me feeling like
I had been swallowed by a snake.
If such a thing would happen
What measures would one take?

I felt as though I was just sitting
In a serpent's belly How to get free?
No one was there to tell me

Pill after pill, night after night
I suffered alone
　　　Thought if there ever was a savior

Nobody's Baby

Then he's already gone

How could it be, why aren't I free?

Why didn't he come and save me?

From the hurt, from the pain

The world has got me in chains

Spending all my days searching for someone to blame

I never wanted to commit suicide

Yet at the same time

I woke up angry every morning cause I'm still alive

Somebody tell me, what is the difference

Told my story over and over

Yet no one paid any attention

Unknowingly, I sold my soul

Over something I felt that I lacked

All my baggage caught up with me

Now I'm forced to unpack or stay crazy

Have you ever broken something while you were only trying to protect it? Perhaps, while trying to protect it you created unnecessary obstacles because you took some extreme measures. To all, that's watching you seem crazy, but the reality is they just don't know what you're holding. They're not aware that what you're carrying is fragile. So over time, you let their questions, opinions, and even their insults get inside your head. You start being a little more careless yet careful all at the same time until finally, you lose yourself and that thing you worked so hard to protect breaks; broken pieces are all that's left for the world to see. What was actually once so valuable is now a bunch of broken parts exposed. Now you spend all your time trying to assure yourself that you were indeed once this valuable thing! Once upon a time, you believed everything God said about you, everything he showed you, you could be. However, over time you allowed the world to convince you of otherwise.

Looking back, I believe I really did love me. The problem was I loved myself the way that I knew how to love. Unfortunately, that way wasn't love at all. My version of love was a twisted dysfunction of comfort and kindness that tended to hurt from time to time. If I wasn't hurting me, then I wasn't loving me and that was my ugly yet very real experience of it all. I tried to be careful with myself and with my life, but I was so careful that I was careless and I made a mess of everything. Throughout my twenties, I could only see what my life should have been instead of seeing what my life could be. I couldn't see what my life could be because I no longer had hope. I guess I figured if this was the way my life was considering what my life has been, surely, it was never going to get any better than what it was right then.

With that mindset, I figured why even bother to wake up at all? There was nothing to wake up and try for. We're all waking up trying for something, isn't that part of what life is about — trying for something? I spent a lot of years trying for nothing because I had given up on everything. I was carrying so much pain on my back. Was I hard-headed? No! I would have been willing to listen, but what do you do when you're young and don't have anyone to guide you? What do you do when your mother needs a mother too?

Nobody's Baby

I know you're thinking things should be getting better for Stacey since she finally escaped from Byron, but she had left something—a lot of things actually. Whenever I was done with anything, I would always just leave it right where it was. I never tried to sort things out or take what I needed and destroy the rest. No, I would always just leave everything. When I tell you these things I don't mean in a physical aspect but more from a psychological one. I wouldn't try to learn from anything. I'd go through life just shelving all my situations, good or bad circumstances. I wasn't experiencing life's many lessons. For me, it was merely tragedy after tragedy. This was the real reason why things seemed so bad for me. Over time I'd learn that there is a peace in receiving the message. There is comfort in the lesson, always!

I ran from what life wanted to teach me because I was afraid life was trying to make me feel, and by now you should know how I felt about feeling anything. I didn't even want to feel good. Things were so dark for me that I was even afraid of feeling too good because feeling good was so uncomfortable. I could never enjoy good feelings because I focused on being aware of how temporary they were that I braced myself for when those good feelings were going to leave. See, I told you from chapter one that I was never in the moment.

Every time I thought I had a plan, just when I thought I could look ahead, it seemed as though things would crumble right before my eyes. Yes, I was free from Byron but I would still spend many years paying for letting him in my life. Yes, London and I were over but I would spend many years with my heart rippling with pain as I battled the pull of our soul tie. Those two things alone were tearing me up but then more got added to it. All I can say is, I tried!

Yvonne Gurley

I tried to be young and go out on the weekends with my friends. I tried the process of dating but my circumstances made even what was so simple and typical for my age almost impossible. When I originally left Byron, I hoped to buy my first home. I had taken a firsttime home buyers' class and gotten a grant. Although things were always getting turned off at home, I was secretly paying debtors off on my credit report. When I left him, I moved my daughter and I into an apartment but I didn't think we'd be there for more than a year. I almost had my car paid off when I received a letter from human resources advising me that I was going to be garnished. I was astounded. I had been working so hard and I couldn't believe this was happening to me. I had been banking with three banks, one for each job—the pharmacy, the insurance company, and my side job of polishing nails. How on earth did this happen?

I'll tell you how. I'll admit that I wasn't paying attention; I had paid so many things off on my credit I had slowed down on checking it so much. Byron knew about my several accounts and he knew all of my information. I found out there were several payday loans out in my name, and they were all gunning for me. Two of my accounts had been maxed out with overdraft already.

I was making pretty good money at the time so I never checked anything. When I left Byron, I could pay my bills very easily, not thinking twice about anything I needed because I would just pay for it. I'm not saying I could splurge and go on shopping sprees, but I wasn't living above my means and I had a good handle on my finances. I find all of this out and realized my check had been cut down due to the garnishment, which meant I had to move out of my apartment since I could no longer afford it. All of the letters warning me of this has been going to the Sunnydale address.

It was so hard for me to leave that apartment. All of my memories with London were there. I got my freedom there. Life was supposed to start over for me there. Things were getting so bad I could barely afford to feed me and my daughter. Remember my high school sweetheart that I mentioned I was trying to get over at the beginning of this story? You know, the Puerto Rican man I had broken up with before I met Byron, well was in town. His father lived close to me so we talked occasionally. After I told him about everything, he began to help me by keeping food in my house. He even went as far as buying my daughter's Christmas presents for me that year.

I needed more help than that though. I told myself I needed a distraction. So, besides abusing my antidepressants I also became very promiscuous around that time. I know that's the last thing I needed to do but I

did. I always tried to warn the guys I dated that I was broken and they need not take me seriously. Some listened to this warning and some did not. A few put forth their best efforts to try to save me but I could not be saved. Ultimately, they just ended up giving or spending a lot of money on me, which I used for the crises of a situation.

The Puerto Rican guy would continue to try for years but nothing would ever come from his efforts as I wouldn't let it. During this time, I had run into the "wolf," the hot guy I told you from school that I had seen years ago at my old apartment. I saw him on a night I was out on the town and gave him my number. We only talked when he randomly called me one night and asked if he could come by and give me a hug. I thought it was strange and that he was full of it. Nonetheless, I still let him come by. He called me to say he was outside in the parking lot so I met him there. I don't know how he knew I needed a hug, but he did. He hugged me and then he got back into his car and left. That was that. I wouldn't see or hear from him for some time after that.

Once I got into my new apartment, the ship I was on continued to sink. I concluded that I was going to have to file for bankruptcy. There was no way I could pay the banks and all of those payday loans off, not to mention everything else that was on my credit I had been working on. I was forty thousand dollars in debt! When I reached out to Byron about what he had done he openly and boldly admitted to it and stated, "Well, I had to pay my parents back some money and you know how much these bills are at this house. Man, I needed the money." Typical Byron looking out for himself and not considering the fact that our daughter lives with me and he had just made life extremely hard for us.

I did not have any peace in my new apartment either. I had running toilets and a stopped-up sink, plus my thermostat was broken so it was always cold as the air never turned off. I would complain to management but they would never fix a thing. My life just kept getting messier and messier by the minute.

I was used to being spiritually broken and perhaps even mentally broken but now I was financially broke, too. I carried on with my promiscuous ways and lost the little grip I had on my pill taking. Though I had made a little progress after what the stripper, Adrian had done, my circumstances swallowed me whole and I nosedived. I decided you at least deserved to know Adrian's' name after what he had done. Clearly, he was more than a stripper. I didn't ever go back to those particular pills he had flushed that had such a grasp on me for so many years, but at that point, I had a variety of other prescription pills I tried. Because of the condition of my apartment, my water bill in my two-bedroom apartment was running me a whopping four hundred bucks a month, and my electricity bill was neck and neck with it. I was already in the middle of bankruptcy so how do you think I was doing at this time?

Let's add on the fact that I was getting phone calls from my daughter's pre-K school. Byron was the only person I had to go pick her up from school since he wasn't working. This was the one thing I asked him to do just until I got off of work and he couldn't get that right. My daughter's teacher complained that he was showing up late almost every day and sometimes not at all and on those days, I'd have to leave work early. Did I tell you on the days he did bother to show up he appeared to be high? It got so bad that her teacher felt compassion for me; she agreed to just keep my child with her until I got off work, as she was afraid Social Services would be called. I got off work just thirty minutes after her school let out so she didn't have to keep her long which meant Byron didn't have to keep her long but he still couldn't even do that. Again, I was drowning in every way possible.

If you thought it couldn't get any worse, it did! One night the complex decided to work on the water in everyone's building so they had to shut it off. My daughter and I didn't realize this until we attempted to turn the water on. They gave no notice of this work they just did it and left you to figure out that the water was off. It was late so my child and I proceeded to go to sleep. I recall thinking it was raining as in my sleep I heard what sounded like rain all night. However, it was not raining. When I awoke, the floors were all soaked. My entire apartment was flooded. You see, when my daughter attempted to turn the water on, she had no gage of knowing whether or not she had turned it off because they had shut everyone's water off. Because my sinks were stopped up, instead of the water just running down the drain all night it ran over the sink and flooded my entire apartment and the apartment under me. The complex blamed this entire fiasco on me and gave me a huge bill. They filed a lawsuit against me and I was served with papers. I was wrapping up my bankruptcy and it was too late to try to add anything else so I was just stuck in this horrible situation, and I was also a horrible person at that time. I'm not trying to excuse my bad behavior but can you blame me? Dang!

I had no one. Nobody could help me. I was still having panic attacks and nightmares from my childhood and could barely function because my nerves were so bad. Once again I had to move. I stopped paying rent and used it to put down a deposit on another place. Meanwhile, in the midst of all this, I was still partying. Yes, I was broke and partying, all my friends were. I don't think their problems were as bad as mine, but they were also dealing with some major issues of their own. How were we partying with no money? Well, that's easy—we're women. Someone is always willing to pay your way in and even buy everyone drinks. We didn't need money to go out.

I recall one night standing in my kitchen acting out a scene from the John Singleton film, *Baby Boy*. I was making my friend laugh when I stated, "I want somebody who has turned their life around." I was referring to Melvin's' character from the film and I was just joking. My life was very dark then but I would always run to humor. I enjoyed making my friends laugh but it was only to hide how hurt I was from everything. Funny though, after I made this statement, I get a phone call from Wolf. I hadn't heard from him in almost a year. I had run into him at the club and he asked for my number again. We hung out a few times but I had entirely too much going on to give anybody my time.

Wolf made me feel a way I cannot describe. I was always uncomfortable around him. He made my heart race. No one had ever made me feel that way or come close. London had a similar effect on me but the way Wolf made me feel was different. The feeling London gave made me want to run to him and never let go. Wolf made me want to run from him and never look back. Yea I know, I'm so dramatic. Wolf wanted to know me; a lot of people did but I just wouldn't let them in. I didn't just act this way with men; I did it with my female friends, too. If I felt they were getting too close I stopped hanging out with them. I wouldn't call or answer any phone calls or reply to texts. I didn't want anyone in.

Leading up to my last days in that apartment, my depression went to a place it had never gone before. I had run out of distractions. I ran to the gas station and bought a few black and mild's, even though I wasn't a smoker—I needed something. It plagued me because I couldn't figure out what I needed. I sat in my room at my computer desk and lit a candle, turned the music on, and zoned out as I smoked. I went to my closet where I had hidden the returned letters I received from my attempts in trying to write my father years ago. Staring at the fire from the candle took me to another place. I decided to light the fireplace threw the returned letters in as I laid on the floor and screamed. I kicked and I cried like a baby as I watched those letters burn. He was officially dead to me and I tried to accept that he was never going to come back.

After those letters burned, I went back to my room and sat back down, puffing a little more as I proceeded to stare at the candle once again. If you think my behavior is irrational it's because it was. I sat there alone as tears just kept falling. I was no longer screaming but the tears just kept coming. The weight of everything I was going through and everything I had been through had just sat on me. I finally couldn't run anymore. All those bags of luggage I filled had finally been shipped back to me and I had to deal with everything. I had checked completely out.

Before I knew it, that candle had burned all the way down and had broken the glass jar it was in so my computer desk was on fire. I came to and rushed to quickly put the fire out. All the years of rape and molestation were getting to me. I couldn't get the beatings out of my head. The plague I was living with from having been with Byron and all the repercussions that came from that and my financial problems had me breaking down. There was no amount of therapy, drugs, or sex that was ever going to fix what I was going through, what I was feeling inside.

I titled this chapter "Unpacked" because my life really did unpack on me then. I felt like I had stood in the middle of a crowded room and yelled, "Silence" and, although I succeeded in getting everyone's attention, no one reacted. I wanted someone to do something. I wanted someone, anyone, to say something but they didn't. Instead, they just reacted to the word that I was yelling instead of acknowledging the fact that I was screaming. I wanted them to notice I was screaming and do something about that but all they heard and reacted to was the word,
"Silence!"

Nobody's Baby
All those bags of luggage I filled had finally been shipped back to me and I had to deal with everything.

22   Screams of Silence

How is a distraction to your faith! Before I had found my new place, I really began to question God. I attempted to go to church from time to time but nothing ever came from it. However, I was desperate to be healed. I wanted to be cured of everything that was consuming my life. Though I ran from Wolf, he was special to me. So, I disappeared in efforts not to hurt him. I never contacted Wolf again. Unbeknownst to me, I didn't have to run from Wolf because I'd later find out that he went to prison around that time and would be gone for almost four years. Wolf was very pretty but he was also a bad boy all the way. Yep, he was just my type. Ain't it sad, y'all, just sad!

   I know I mentioned having paid my deposit on my next new place but how I found it was quite remarkable. By my daughter's school, there were these beautiful condos. I always wanted to live in a condo, though I assumed I could never afford one, especially in my current position. I would ride pass those condos every day fantasizing about actually being able to move in. I took my fantasy a little further than most and began to pull into the complex. There was one that was empty and had a for rent sign. I pulled up to that empty condo every single day after picking my daughter up from school. I began to tell my friends about it and how I wished it could be mine, as I saw pictures of the inside. I'd envision how I'd want my furniture to be placed and how my daughter and I would have a nice place to call our own.

I was so used to bad news that I went out on a limb and applied for the condo. I told myself I wouldn't get approved and just did it for the sake of having something to hope for. It was also a distraction for me. Waiting to see if I got approved took my mind off of everything else. My pay was no longer being garnished by that time and my bankruptcy payments were over as well. As it turned out, the rent for the condo was only twenty dollars more than what I was already paying and also had paid water. I held my breath for that entire week for approval, expecting a denial.

When I got the news that I indeed had been approved I couldn't believe it. My bankruptcy had not yet shown up on my credit and neither had my current situation. I was overzealous with my good news. When I moved in, I felt this rush of peace I had never experienced. I never knew such a feeling even existed. I was so in love with the serene feeling that I never wanted to leave home. No, really! When I moved into that condo I would never leave unless I had to. I'd go to work and grab my daughter on the way home and not leave until I had to do it all over again.

Nobody's Baby

That was when I started to feel paranoid like it wasn't safe anywhere but in my home, and especially in my room. It wasn't just me but everyone who visited me would rave about how peaceful it felt and would make statements about not wanting to leave this mysterious peaceful presence. It got to the point where my friends and family would call and want to come over after a bad day just desperate to feel the tranquility that awaited them in my condo. Words cannot describe the way my new home made me feel. I was protective of it. Honestly, it made me even wackier. I didn't understand this peace but I loved it.

Because I had just experienced so much, even my newfound peace wasn't enough. I spent all of my days paranoid of the next storm that was sure to come. I was afraid to go to sleep and afraid to wake. I knew my dreadful past would be waiting to torture me in my sleep and I knew my future would be waiting for me with its next surprise when I woke up.

I was as paranoid as a person could be; thus, I took more and more pills. I had discovered that wine wasn't as harsh on my stomach and beer wasn't either so I began to chase my pills with either of the two. My nerves were so shot that I'd keep a small personal bottle of wine in the armrest of my car. While at work, I'd frequently run out to my car and chase a pill with a swig of alcohol. If you're beginning to think I was losing it, I was! I wasn't sleeping, I was barely eating—I was hardly functioning at all. I was so, so very tired; I didn't have any fight left in me. PTSD is hard to fight, especially without God. This mental illness literally won't let you let go or get over your past; no matter how bad you want to.

My family had convinced me that nothing ever happened to me and that bothered me so much. I began to doubt myself. Was I indeed crazy and had just made up my entire childhood? If I did make everything up, then why did I have these scars? I had all the scars on my body from all those brutal nights I endured. I still suffered from headaches because of the blow I took to my left eye. I still had the many scars on my legs from the night I was kicked repeatedly. I still found myself leaving my body every time I laid with someone new during my promiscuous stage as, somehow, I was trying to conquer my sexual abuse with more sex because I was the one choosing. I wasn't being forced, no one was making me do anything, but I was using sex as a means to conquer this demon I was feeding. Each time I had sex with a new person, I remember always rolling over and crying myself to sleep or running in the shower to cry, as I was raping myself over and over again. I became a completely different person. How do you recognize someone you never knew? You can't! I wanted to know who I was, but I couldn't find me so I just gave up and let life consume me.

Then one day a coworker had invited me to her church. Although I was in this drastic state, I agreed to go. I had shown up late, as I was late for everything. I recall walking in in the middle of service; her pastor stopped preaching as soon as I walked in and focused his eyes on me and then called me up to the altar. That's right, he stopped in the middle of his sermon and called me straight to the altar as soon as I walked in. He embraced me and he began to weep almost uncontrollably. He then proceeded to instruct everyone in this tiny church to hug me. I was confused. I had never witnessed or experienced anything like this before.

After service, he told me that when I walked in God had shown him my entire life and everything I had gone through, which was the reason for all the tears. I didn't know God like that or that such a thing was even possible, so I was even more confused. Part of me wanted to be relieved, as the pastor apologized to me for my sufferings, even though he didn't owe me a thing. Yet, I couldn't be relieved because if he was confirming all these things truly happened to me, I was even more hurt wondering why on earth did someone who loved me let all those awful things happen to me while I was a child. Why didn't my family, my friends, or anybody save me? My biggest question was if God saw everything then why didn't he save me? I couldn't wrap my mind around it.

My perception was distorted. You see, when I was repeatedly being raped, molested, and beaten God was there. When I went through my addiction and being promiscuous, he was there. As I've stated, when God gave us free will, he didn't say sometimes. Therefore, when someone decides to be a monster, they are using their free will to do such things just as much as someone choosing to do good. My abuse was never his fault, my bad choices were never his fault and neither my sin nor the world's sin equals his abandonment of me or you.

Yvonne Gurley

When I thought I left him, he did everything he could until I could see He never left me! For some people, God has to make them rich or famous or make this grand gesture for them to see his presence but for me, all God had to show me was that I was still alive! He had to reveal my life and ultimately my freedom to me because I had believed I was dead. When you've been violated there's something inside you that breaks and no amount of words can describe the transformation of your spirit when it happens. When this violation happened on more than one occasion, for me my spirit had to die in order for me to live.

I made peace with my feelings about God but it still took some time for me to fully understand his presence in my life and what that looked like and what it meant. I refocused my hurt feelings back to my mother. I couldn't understand how my mother could allow such cruelty to be inflicted on her child or worse, be one of the inflictors. I may have in some ways become her but the one thing I could never do was be violent to my child. I was so afraid that the same monster lived inside me that I hardly ever disciplined her at all.

After many years of being an abuser of my prescription drugs, I realized my mother behaved like a typical addict. You see, I only knew and experienced two sides of her—either she was overly kind and passive due to being high, or she was mean, angry, and violent due to the lack of her pills. It was the only version my siblings and I ever had of our mother. Nonetheless, I still couldn't understand why she allowed or did such things to me

Nobody's Baby

and my siblings. My feelings of not being loved became even more overwhelming after that realization.

I drowned deeper and deeper into my pain as if such a place could go any further. I began to try this church thing out with my coworker (who became my friend) but it was so difficult for me. I didn't feel loved there either. I felt like everyone saw a fractured woman and judged me for it. No one hardly spoke to me, even at times when I'd just be sitting in a pew after church crying my eyes—no one bothered to ask what was wrong. Instead, they would all just carry on and congregate in the frontal space while leaving me in the sanctuary to cry alone, just like I did at home. This was a very small church, not even twenty people attended yet no one felt compelled to see about me. They only whispered and judged for my inconsistency in attendance.

The pastor would often instruct everyone to find somebody to hug and I can recall just like it was yesterday how it was obvious husbands were instructed to stay clear of me. Certain people would make it a point to hug everyone but me. I could see if I came to church dressed provocatively or behaved in a flirtatious manner, but it was none of the sort. On the days I did muster up the strength to make it in, I was desperate, but not for anybody's man—I was desperate to know God. After London, to my knowledge, I never involved myself in an affair again of any sorts. No matter how bad I was hurting, I never wanted to feel the way being in an affair makes you feel. I discovered the person who participated in affairs was never me at all. I didn't like her and her character was useless to me. Now that I'm more spiritually mature I'm aware that what's in your spirit can tell on you. I don't take personal at all the distance. I even recall the Pastor making an announcement that the spirit of Jezebel was in the church. I at the time had no idea what that meant at all. Looking back the proper thing to do would have been to pray for me, perhaps speak to me privately, and educate me, show me that I was in a spiritual battle and assure me I didn't have to fight alone. I knew nothing about generational curses, this Jezebel spirit, or anything. When I decided to fight this invisible battle, the enemy kept sending married men my way. They were always approaching me but I fought back. Even if a guy had a girlfriend I still fought because God convinced me the woman operating under that spirit was not me.

The pastor had given the notion that God wasn't in fact gone as I thought, but that he was real, very real. I was eager to find out how to get to Him. I just wanted to get some messages across but I didn't know how. It took everything I had not to fall apart every Sunday that I attended. So, when the congregation treated me this way all it did was add insult to my many injuries. I'm aware I had a past and I'm also aware of my behavior but by that time in my life I was so tired and strung out on prescriptions, I couldn't see straight. The last thing I was ever thinking about was somebody's man at church. Once again, just like with my family, my friends, and now with the church, I found myself screaming "SILENCE" and everyone's reaction was the same—looking at me but no one understanding that I was screaming.

On a particular day, I was so beside myself that I randomly got up in the middle of my shift and just left work. I didn't say anything to anyone, I didn't clock out—I just got up and left. I drove all the way home and I couldn't begin to tell you how I got there. I'm not even sure if I went straight there. All I know is I was being awoken by a friend of mine as she was screaming and shaking me like crazy. As I came to, she hugged me having thought the worse had happened. Everyone knew of my reckless behavior so naturally, she thought I had finally succumbed to it. She stated that the daycare had called her because I did not pick my child up, which wasn't like me. Since her kids attended the daycare as well, the staff called her knowing we were friends. My friend then proceeded to tell me when she pulled up to my house my front door was wide open and she found me lying face down. She tried calling my name but when I gave her no response she panicked, as it took a few hard shakes to get me up. I apologized to her for the scare and her having to pick my daughter up. Unfortunately, I then had the nerve to make a sarcastic joke: "Oh, you thought I was dead? Honey, please. Listen, people like me don't get to get out of here. Instead, we just remain tortured souls while people with good lives get to die. No, I'm stuck here as some sort of a cruel joke that I desperately try to find the humor in." My friend, understanding my sarcastic humor, found my statement just as funny as I did.

Yvonne Gurley

I didn't take my erratic behavior serious at all. None of my actions was a precaution to me. I continued my dangerous cocktail of pills, alcohol, and occasionally marijuana. I also kept subjecting myself to the judgment I felt every Sunday I attempted to go to church and find the Lord. I really wanted to talk to him and I was just trying to get his number. I knew I didn't care for the church itself as I felt they could never help me anyway; I was going strictly to get to the source. I was not getting any sleep again because my body had grown accustomed to my many cocktails and nothing would allow me to fall asleep. I had been up for days and started hallucinating.

My tortured past was louder than ever. I took pill, after pill, after pill and drank, and drank, and drank. Finally, I had fallen asleep and the dream I had was worse than any dream I had before. I had dreamed I had slit my throat in front of my then four-year-old daughter. The dream was so morbid and realistic that it frightened me. I woke up immediately and began to cry. I cried so hard that there was no way I was going to try to go back to sleep. Instead, I attempted to talk to the one the church called God. I cried out to Him and began explaining myself, telling him how I would never do such a thing. I'd never commit suicide let alone do something so tragic and force my child to bear witness. As I explained these things out loud, talking to someone I could not see, to my surprise, a voice seemed to speak from inside me. He asked me if I was sure about what I claimed. He asked me if I was sure I'd never do this to my child. He asked me how I knew I wasn't doing that very thing he had just shown me.

I thought about it as I grabbed my chest and gasped for air that had seemed so thin. He was right! The voice that spoke from within me made me see clearly as no one had done before. I was indeed killing myself right before my daughter's eyes. I didn't realize that, though I was doing it slowly and quietly, I was actually quite loud and still dying in front of her just as tragically.

I knew what I had to do. I did what should have been done many years ago. I pulled myself together as much as I could and got my daughter off to school. Then I went back home and cried some more. Finally, I texted my sister to come to get me. She replied, "Come get you? Why, where you at?"

That, my darlings, are all the ways I found myself lying on the bathroom floor and on my way to Brightway, the mental health hospital!

Therefore, when someone decides to be a monster, they are using their free will to do such things just as much as someone choosing to do good. My abuse was never his fault, my bad choices were never his burdens, and my sin, nor the world's sin, equal his abandonment of me or you.

23 Junk

I prayed to God with my mask on wondering why things still went wrong. When you're hurt, you wear a mask all day, even when you're alone or praying. I went to the Lord but not as my true self begging and pleading for help. I vowed to the world that I would never cry, never reveal my pain. I would rather lie. Yet I wondered why I felt the way I did inside.

When you're broken, you feel like the worst thing you can do is let anyone know that you're broken. I refer to this as wearing a mask. I got so good at hiding my emotions that even when I wanted to cry, I couldn't. When something made me happy I could never really enjoy or feel the happiness. I could only smile, and even that wasn't real. It was as if I had some sort of a block and all I knew or was capable of was this one middle ground feeling; however, this wasn't a feeling, it was only being numb.

I was so determined to wear my mask that when I was alone and free to be myself, I still wouldn't take it off. I didn't even want to reveal my pain to myself. I wanted to be free from things I wasn't willing to face. The only way to overcome anything is to face it. Looking back, I guess I just wanted some magic to happen. I wanted my past to not be my past and I wanted my present to be anything but what it was. Then I wanted my future to be so many things that I wasn't willing to work for at the time. What's worse was my life was everybody's fault but mine.

How could I be so angry at the world and even at God for treating me according to what I exposed? I was depending on God to read my mind and to know how much I needed him. I did this with people, too. I was afraid that exposing myself would make me look weak and I certainly couldn't have that. In my head, weak people definitely were treated poorly and I had enough of that already. However, what I didn't realize was wearing a mask was weak and was one of the feeblest things I could do, which was the reason for everything.

So, after years of suffering from depression, anxiety, medication, and therapy, I realized something—nothing worked because I approached everything with my mask on. The moment I removed my mask and revealed my true self, then I could begin to really get to know myself. Then I started to figure out what was hurting and why I was hurting. From that it allowed me to go to God with what I really needed. The moment I opened my mouth my true healing began. So, if this sounds like you, take your mask off as fast as you can!

I was finally going to deal with the unfinished business in my life, all my junk! Your junk is all the stuff you don't want to deal with—everything and anything that you put away and told yourself you'd return to but never did. Guess what happens when that closet gets full? It starts spilling over and before you know it that closet door can no longer close and you're looking for new places to hide your junk. However, when you've run out of closets and you don't have a choice but to leave your junk out in the open that is where the danger kicks in because you're exposed and you have to be careful. You have to watch your step because you're trying not to trip over your own junk and the people who are in your life end up watching out for your junk, too!

While encouraging myself, I would like to inspire others to "deal with it." Whatever your "it" may be, deal with each and every one of them. No matter how big or small, face everything. Life really and truly is what you make it. You are the judge of the size of your problems. To truly believe that nothing is too hard for God means that all of your problems should weigh the same. Give everything to God and let your faith remain.

While I was in Brightway, I was forced to talk. I didn't at first but the other patients made me aware that the only way to ever get out was to talk and fully participate in everything. I tried to spend my days there in my room lying in bed in the dark but the staff quickly let me know there would be none of that.

I had indulged in too many movies that took place in a mental health hospital. I assumed I would be drugged up to my entire stay but I was wrong. As soon as I was processed was when the fun began. I learned what being crazy really looked like and I didn't quite fit that category as well as I thought. I witnessed a patient yelling at the staff to give him a shot. When the nurses refused, he proceeded to run his head into the wall, banging his head over and over until there was blood. Then he got exactly what he was asking for as well as strapped down and sent to another unit. That patient wasn't really out of his mind; he just didn't want to be released. He didn't want to go back into the world where he had to face the realization that he had nothing and nobody. He didn't want to be reminded that he was "nobody's baby." I couldn't blame him, none of us wanted to face that feeling so he would do himself harm; sounds and looks familiar doesn't it! I only know this because he had confessed these feelings to all of us, patients, while on a smoke break. I didn't smoke but I went on every single smoke break for the interesting talks.

Just like in the movies, the patients were forced to participate in exercises where we had to imagine we were a tree or a bird or something even more absurd. When I saw this was the upcoming activity, I refused and I ran out of the room. The staff asked what was wrong and I stated I wasn't going to participate. They told me I had to but I again refused. I replied, "If you want me to do what they're doing in there, then you have to give me whatever it is you gave them." The staff nearly fell down with laughter.

Even though I had previously had what some would call a spiritual experience, I brushed it off. I took the voice from within as just part of my hallucinations. It took me a while to realize it was God. I was called in for a personal counseling session while everyone else did the silly exercises. After pouring my heart out, the psychologist told me I wasn't crazy. The staff did not believe I was

mentally ill and did not medicate me at all the entire time I was there. In a way, I was pissed. The psychologist stated, "Why Stacey, I'm afraid that if these events [my abuse] did indeed occur, you have every right to feel exactly how you've been feeling. In fact, if you didn't have these emotions I'd be more concerned. You don't need
medication at all, I'm afraid you never did."

We had group counseling sessions in which we discussed what led us to our breaking points. The floor I was on was co-ed. My roommate had already told me her story and revealed she was a frequent patient of the facility. She was there merely for a broken heart; her husband had spent their entire marriage being a repeat offender of unfaithfulness. Every time she felt he was off with his mistress she would check herself in. The pain was just too much for her to bear alone and she couldn't find the strength to leave him. She cried a lot. In fact, she cried so much that I was glad when she was transferred to another room because she didn't like sleeping directly under a vent. In turn, I had the room all to myself and I was glad. All of her cries made me even more depressed.

There was a guy there who shared his story. He opened up by asking us if we thought he looked like "The Nutty Professor." We all stated no as we were all too knee deep in our pain to think on that level. He began to share that so many people told him that he did that he started to believe it. He also shared how he was plagued with guilt because he felt responsible for his family's crackcocaine addiction. He went to college to play football in the eighties. At the time he was residing in Los

Angeles, California and when he went home to visit his family while on a break from school he saw how much money his cousins and uncles were making from dealing crack. He was so intrigued that he gave his football scholarship up and didn't think twice about going back to school. He started dealing and before he knew it he had his entire family hooked on drugs. This tortured him and he blamed himself, not allowing his truth to go. He felt so bad about that he requested shock therapy.

I heard many more stories, some less tragic though some more. There was a girl who was found in the park with a rope around her neck attempting suicide. She was found in time to bring her back to consciousness and over to the hospital. She still had the rope imprints around her neck, which made looking at her depressing. She shared that she had been severely sexually abused as a child; the memories of that wouldn't stop haunting her and it was affecting her marriage. She thought her husband and kids would be better off without her. I was shocked again as I didn't think African American women even thought to hang themselves. Why was I so shocked? Our culture has always been conditioned to suffer in silence.

There was also a young man that had been transferred from jail to our unit. He wanted out as well, but not out of confinement—out of life. The police had been called in after people witnessed him trying to jump off of a bridge. He never said why he was so sad but I knew he made threats to kill himself quite often to staff as well as the people he would call on the phone. I later realized it was not that he wanted out so bad he just needed proof and reassurance that he mattered. He needed to know every single day that somebody in this world cared about him. I couldn't blame him, isn't that what we all need? He would play the role of a tough guy but would cry like a little boy too. I hate seeing black men cry. Our culture has painted a picture of such actions being permitted. It has never been made clear on when exactly it is okay to cry. It's always shocking to bear witness of a man's tears.

Then there was the patient who touched me the most. I'll never forget when he came in wearing his brokenness on the outside. We were all on a smoke break when he arrived and when he came out we all just froze. We tried not to stare at him but his condition made it quite hard. We already had the woman with the rope marks around her neck and now we had this poor young man with cuts all over his body. He was so scarred that his appearance instantly brought us to tears. He was found out in the woods during some sort of military training. We assumed someone else had cut him up but this young man had done it to himself. He told us he couldn't take it anymore. He explained how he was being bullied and the military training reminded him of his past that he was trying desperately to get away from. He poured his heart out to us about growing up in group homes and being sexually and physically abused. He joined the military as a means to escape his painful past but all the military did was remind him of it. He felt as though he was being bullied and had a hard time making friends. So, he made the decision to go out into the woods and end his life. By the time he finished his story, we were all crying. I never met anyone so fragile in my life. I hugged him and he just broke down in tears in my arms. We did our best to comfort him.

Then there was the final patient—me! I wrote and I wrote and I wrote as that was the only thing I was allowed to do besides talk in therapy. I couldn't remember ever going that many days without some sort of a substance since before I met Byron. I have to admit I was beginning to feel good. My sisters had even come to visit me. My daughter had been staying with them. They were alternating he care of her. When they came for visits, they were very emotional and in tears and explained to me how brave they thought I was being for finally facing my demons. I gave myself permission to let my heartbreak.

The truth had made another attempt to visit and I finally let him in. Oh, how I fell in love with the truth during my stay. I began to dig deep and think as hard as I could about all of my truths, which no longer had to hunt me down. I was actually on my own journey to find my truth, but we would play this game for more years to come.

Leading up to the final days of my stay, I met my childhood friend's aunt. She hugged me and told me I was still her niece though I hadn't seen her in years. She was very kind and I was very embarrassed and ashamed, especially since she worked there. I thought back and wondered if she or my childhood friends' mother knew just how much she had saved me from all those nights and days I spent in her home.

As I prepared for my final therapy session, my doctor told me how proud she was of me and all of my progress. She also stated she believed if I stuck to my journey of truths and healing that I had it in me to help so many people with my writing, which I often shared with the staff who thought I had so much talent. I thought to myself, "Well, if being broken is equivalent to having talent, then yea I've got a lot of that." I was approved to go home and I have yet to ever go back!

I gave myself permission to have a broken heart.

24 Predictions

There is no healing in the truths which we deny. My truth was I had the potential to have such a full life despite my past, my brokenness, or my shortcomings. The other truth was my denial of it actually happening. If you try to predict your own unhappiness it is sure to come, not by predetermined bad conditions though; for example, a person would know he or she would be miserable if left stranded in a desert, whereas if a person assumes he or she will be miserable on a new job, then misery is preconceived due to lack of evidence of the job. Ultimately, the experience ends up however you predicted it would.

The followers of Christ in the scriptures could have fallen into miserable situations with the preconceived mindset that their conditions would overtake them and they would surely die but they didn't. Instead, they trusted God in every circumstance and every condition they were thrown into. Misery cannot live where it is not wanted, neither can faith. I just wish young Stacey would have known that back then.

Nobody's Baby

When I left Brightway, I think I may have had hope. I wasn't anywhere close to having faith or even fully grasped the meaning of faith, but I certainly didn't know the difference between the two. However, I know it seemed like I had this huge awakening, it had seemed that way for me, too. Didn't the details of my experience give you hope as well? I admit that's what it gave me but unfortunately, that was all it gave me. I didn't leave Brightway a healed person. I'm afraid there is no psych ward on this planet I could have gone to that would have had the power to do that. When I checked myself in I was sad and a few other things. When I left there, I was simply in a better mood. To me now, faith is the belief in your hopes carried through, be it by your own efforts or something far greater than you!

I had hope that I could actually have a better life but I didn't believe it could happen. With that being said, I was in denial of the possibilities of my own happiness. I wanted things to be better but I predicted they never would be. As I've learned the way life works, whatever you believe does everything it can to prove itself to be true. Like how I wanted to believe London wasn't married, for over a year it seemed like he really wasn't because I saw only what I believed. However, just because you believe it, just because you think you see it, doesn't mean it's reality. In fact, it may only be real to you. My life was the way it was because I gave it the power to be. Over the years I would learn to be careful what to give power to as I had always given power to my bad circumstances, mistakes, and flaws. Brightway showed me that whatever I felt I needed healing from would never be found in those pills, as they made clear I never needed them. However, they didn't show me how I could be healed; thus, my hope with no faith. In other words, I left happy but I also left tired and broken still. I needed a cure.

"A cheerful heart is a good medicine, but a broken spirit saps a person's strength."
Proverbs 17:22 NLT

London had learned of my stay at Brightway and shown so much concern while I was away, I advised my sister to let him know I was alright. I appreciated his efforts to care, I really did. Even after we ended things, no matter how much time had gone by when he'd hear of any misfortunes, he'd always try to make sure I knew he cared. Before London, I had always felt like a tumbleweed to everyone else in my life. In the past, I tested the boundaries of London's love as often as I could just trying to get him to show me how much he loved me. I did this over and over again. His efforts to demonstrate this grand love would prove to never be good enough. What once filled a void in me created a void someplace else over time. I used to press all of London's buttons like a child to a parent who felt wasn't getting enough attention. I acted out with him, he acted out with me, and I grew tired of our games. On one hand, I'd say that this man couldn't possibly have ever loved me because he would have never lied to me and he would have never asked me to be in a position that I would one day be ashamed and embarrassed about. Then, on the other hand, I'd say, given his brokenness, it is possible that in his mind he really did love me the best way that he could even if it was morally wrong. It would never be morally wrong in his eyes because London didn't believe in God.

London seemed to teleport to my side after I told him I was home. We talked all night about my experience and even shared some laughs about it. We caught up as we hadn't talked or seen each other in quite a while. We must have talked ourselves right to sleep as I don't recall anything else. The next morning I awoke to some strange noise that seemed to be coming from above my head. As I opened my sleepy eyes I couldn't believe what I was seeing. Big and tall London was standing on my bed carving his name into the wall above me with a knife. I jumped up and screamed. I begged him to stop but he kept going. He went from wall to wall carving his name over and over again. He yelled back at me as I yelled at him. He was angry with me for leaving him and had grown frustrated while I was away. He was also angry because we were no longer. As he continued to carve his name he told me if his name was in every wall there was no way I could ever have anyone else over. He didn't want to be replaced. I could no longer hear what he was saying as my mind went into another place.

My PTSD was in full swing. Before I knew it, I went and I grabbed a hammer. I knew to be only five-feet-three inches as London stood six-feet-two that I was no match for his strong arms. I grabbed the hammer and as I proceeded toward him, feeling my heart exploding. The tears streamed down my face as I begged him, "Please don't make me use this. Please don't make me hit you."

London became even angrier and grabbed an iron from the hall closet; he launched it at me from across the living room of my tiny condo. I made up my mind at that moment that I was fully prepared to fight him until death, even if it meant the death of us both. I began chasing him around the room swinging the hammer as hard and as fast as I could. We were both screaming at the top of our lungs. He proceeded to carve his name one last time in another wall and this time my swing came close enough to show him that I had every intention of contacting his face with my hammer. I came so close that we both immediately went into shock as we realized just how close we were to really hurt each other. We concluded it was time for him to go after that.

I felt like God and the Devil were officially at war over me. My soul felt like it was being pulled in different directions. I was filled with rage and I needed somebody to tell me, despite it all, I was worth something. Although I had been raped, molested, battered, and abused, I was still worth something. I needed to matter to somebody. I required for everything bubbling inside me to matter to someone other than me.

London proved to me at that moment that he was just as broken as me and my healing couldn't come from him either. In that last fight, I gave up on him being the hero he once was for so long. I needed to know I was still beautiful on the inside. When you are violated in such a way, you feel like your insides are ugly. What in the world was I going to do with ugly insides? They don't make cosmetics for that, you know. There is no plastic surgery or medicine to cure the scars made from within. I needed for somebody to see me, really see me, and tell me I was priceless.

For so long I would ask every guy I dated why he liked me. In the past, whenever London would tell me he loved me I'd always reply, "You do?" I had grown dependent on the world to tell me what my value was because I didn't know. I never knew. It was never taught to me, amongst so many other things. Brightway didn't give me that nor had my past relationships with men or women I befriended—nothing I had previously experienced could give me what I was desperately searching for.

No one cared because I was beautiful, or so they thought. Hollywood movies are always showing what the world deems as unattractive to be the people who get mistreated the most, but that couldn't be further from the truth. I was an adorable child and I paid the price for it, like so many of you did too. I got no sympathy from women because they judged me based on the fact that I always had a good-looking guy on my arm. They judged my fake smile, well-put-together attire, and nice hair. They judged everything they thought they saw on the outside and had nothing to offer me. I can recall a time I was crying at work during one of my many trials with Byron and my supervisor seemed so surprised; she stated, "Now why are you crying? You're too pretty to be in here crying." Why does the world think attractive people have no pain? It's like someone took away the rights to cry.

Yvonne Gurley

As you can see, I was right back to swirl in my misery, but this time I was doing it sober. I felt everything and I hated every second of it. I thought about taking a pill but as I got ready to put the pill to my mouth that voice that seemed to speak from within was back. It spoke again. I had put that entire experience out of my mind. This time I was sober so I knew I wasn't hallucinating or just high. The voice was so clear and stern, like the voice of a father to a daughter. I reacted as such and immediately put the pill down. To this very day, I have never even attempted to take pills again. After that moment, I got in my bed and confessed my pain aloud. Everything I was feeling on the inside I said out loud. I just needed to get what was in, out! I didn't have any more room left. I spoke from the pit of my heart, not knowing or even fathoming anyone was indeed listening.

I tried to pick up the pieces to return to work and my dysfunctional social life but I was different. I struggled to adjust to being sober all day every day. I had tried church and I still felt empty like this shell whenever I went. I had run into a classmate who offered for me to join her circle of friends. This new group of women turned out to be both good and bad for me. They were independent career women who smiled to my face but whispered behind my back. All but two of the women quickly showed me I wasn't good enough to be in their presence. I saw right through my classmate and I let her know about it after a trip we took to Miami. I remember after being the first one to finish getting ready to go out to the club one of the ladies made the comment, "Not everybody looks like a celebrity" in reference to me. I chuckled knowing many people said I looked like somebody famous. Dozens of people thought I was the brown-skinned girl that graced television when in reality I did not look like any of them. Even Byron and London thought I looked like an actress. When I tell you I always looked like somebody to people, I did but I guess I just had common features. This instance got on my nerves because once again I was being mistreated by women because of what they thought they saw on the outside when I was hurting so severely on the inside.

Not long after the trip, my car was running on its last leg. Over the years, the only maintenance I could ever afford were oil changes so all of the other incomplete maintenance work finally caught up with me. I managed to get another car without an issue since, after having filed bankruptcy, I paid off my car and my credit was actually pretty good. However, when I went to get my license plates for the car I was informed of an unpaid tax balance. Somehow, I was responsible for the property taxes on Byron's Cadillac, which he hadn't paid in three years, plus my own taxes on the new car. I contacted Byron and informed of the entire situation and his response was, "That's what you get for leaving me. I'm not giving you anything." I had to apply for three credit cards to pay for all the taxes but it put me right back in debt. I had to pay the huge balance from my previous apartment, three credits cards, and a car note every month. Once again, I felt as though I couldn't win. I needed a distraction or at least I thought I did. I didn't run to pills so you guessed it, I ran to a man.

I had gotten an instant message from a guy I dated way back when I was sixteen, Bryce. I only went on one date with him but I never forgot him. We began to talk and we were both excited we found one another as we hadn't seen or spoken to each other in ages. I'll never forget the first time he came over to my place because the strangest thing happened. I had left him downstairs while I was upstairs finishing the final touches on my hair. When I finished and went downstairs, he was wiping my television off. The man was dusting! I teased him about it and we laughed. However, this wasn't what was strange.

The lights in my place started flashing on and off. Now, anytime you see the lights flash on and off in a scary movie it has never turned out to be Jesus! I should have known something wasn't right but I didn't. I let that go as well.

There I was caught right back up in another start of a "circumstantial love." By that time, we had spent countless weeks on the phone with one another and what seemed to be all day every day outside of working hours. When he came over that night, we were so mesmerized. We talked and shared everything, picking right back up like we never left. On that one date we had back when we were sixteen, I had openly admitted to him that I was being abused and his response to my openness scared me away, and I think it scared him away from me as well. He would later reveal to me that it alarmed him because he was being abused, too. So, when we finally got back together it seemed magical. I thought he was special and he reciprocated those same feelings as we drifted off to sleep—but sleep didn't last long for me.

I had dreamed that London was standing at the foot of my bed, so I woke up and sat up as fast as I could. I then had this eerie feeling he was under the bed; once I confirmed he wasn't actually in my room or house, I laid back down but I couldn't go back to sleep. What about the writings on the wall you ask? That was the worst thing he could have done because I had just gotten out of a mental hospital. Of course, everyone thought I came home and really lost my marbles and blamed me for it. My daughter even had an opinion. She stated, "How come London can put his artwork on the wall but if I do it, I get in trouble?" After proving to my family I wasn't the one who did such a thing, I sanded down the many carvings of his name and painted over them.

I had no expectations of my life getting better and, for a long time, it didn't. I was right back in the messy spiral called my life. I went back to distracting myself from my pain with men. The only difference was I wasn't taking pills anymore. Life was exactly what I predicted it to be!

There is no healing in the truths for which we deny.

25 Protection

Before I go any further, I want to take a moment to make it clear that I in no way, shape, or form want to give the impression that London was alone in his crazy. I was crazy too, we just displayed it in different ways. I acted out with words and mind games while he acted out in other ways. But I pulled my own stunts as well when it came to our many battles. Because of this, Bryce thought I needed protection from London. It made me look innocent yet I wasn't because I used words and mind games Bryce couldn't see; he only could see what London was doing to me. To him, London was the bad guy and to London's wife, I was the only bad girl. The truth was London and I did need protection from each other but we also needed protection from ourselves. Up until now, we struggled to break the cycle we were in. We hurt anyone who dared to love us during the time of our dealings with one another.

You see, we didn't want to be together. I know it sounds crazy but it's true, we didn't. We knew if we actually got together, we'd most likely kill each other. As

Nobody's Baby

I explained previously, we were not about romance or a physical attraction; we were attached because of our common psychological issues which made us codependent on each other. He was the one person whom I felt really saw me and he felt like I saw him and there was nobody else on the planet who could ever get that close to either of us. The world would see the made-up version of me, the person I became when I stepped foot outside my home. However, London saw the woman who sat in front of her television with her glasses on, which few people even knew she wore. He knew the girl who had her note pad taking notes while watching "Oprah's Super Soul Sunday." He knew the woman who was always soul searching and could care less about being beautiful, or men, or money. London knew the soul that dwelled within wanting to be free. I never wanted or meant to hurt anybody; I just wanted to be free. London wanted to be free as well. We hurt a lot of people on our quest for freedom. I know it's difficult to fully understand, as I didn't share London's story with you. Just know he indeed had his own pain. We used to live in a world where we only knew the address too. He understood my thought process and I understood his. I'd feel so weird and awkward around everyone but him. I'd confess how I felt about something and he'd always make me feel like my feelings were rational and he totally understood. We were aliens. We agreed we never felt we belonged—not just around people but the planet. No matter the crowded rooms we'd enter we'd both always still felt alone.

Yvonne Gurley

We escaped a lot. Sometimes we'd get away without physically going anywhere. We'd escape in our minds, though not with substances, just with thoughts. We went on many adventures as London was a writer, too. He loved my stories; there's not a poem, song, or idea that he did not read or listen to. We imagined stories and took off with them. There was one time we were on the road and passed by a lot of farmland with cows scattered across the field. I was staring out the window as we drove by when London took one glance at me and stated, "Ok, you're in your head again. What story are you coming up with this time?" I could do nothing but smile as he was totally right. I wasn't present in the moment, but all in my head, as I told you from the beginning that I do. He jumped right in on my game. He said, "You know what? I wonder if the cows know what their fate is," and I excitedly replied, "Right, like I wonder if they've made up this story that they tell one another about this place that every cow goes to but never comes back." He then stated, "Yea, like they probably think they're going somewhere good. They'd have to think they're going somewhere good because when each cow leaves, they never come back." I said, "Exactly! They probably spend their entire lives excited about this place just waiting for their turn to go somewhere that's so great that no one ever returns." Now I know that was a bit out of the left field but that was us—me and London.

There was another incident where we partied so hard the night before that we woke up still in the car at someone's house, who we did not know, just randomly parked in their driveway. I recall waking up in shock that morning and tapped London to get him up. "London, whose house is this?" I asked. He responded, "Oh shoot, I don't know!" He hurried up and pulled out of the driveway and we drove away laughing until we could laugh no more. It was lucky for us we pulled up in the wee hours of the morning after they were asleep and before they could wake up and see us sleeping.

So, do you see how young Stacey thought she could never live without the one person she thought understood her? She couldn't believe London was the same person she needed protection from. We were friends; at least we thought we were. However, we were also that "it's complicated" status as well. We didn't want to be together we just didn't want to be apart either. If that last statement didn't make sense it's because it doesn't! As I said, we hurt anyone who dared to love us during that time. Soul ties hurt, period!

Did London and I ever end? Yes! London and I finally ended—indefinitely. No more sporadic emails or text. He no longer knew how I was doing or what I was doing and vice versa. Also, it wasn't until this point in time, I had found out about Jamaica and June and I ended what I thought for so many years was a true friendship.

I was angry with everyone. I was angry with the career women I hung out with for judging me. When one of the women openly admitted the worst thing that ever happened in her life was a break-up, I threw my hands up. By that point, I developed a strong grudge against those who seemed to have endured nothing yet were so quick to judge without having a glimpse of real pain.

I felt condemned and judged by these so-called perfect people. I wanted to take them and sit them down in a chair in the middle of a crowded room and let each judgmental person scream while everyone watches them being tortured. Yes, let everyone still carry on like they see or hear nothing yet whisper to each other about the shrieking anguish of the judgmental people. That's it, let everybody watch as you're so clearly being tortured but don't offer any help just whisper and stare.

This was the level of brokenness I had reached. My thoughts went everywhere and I couldn't have been more honest with myself or with God. It was new to me. I liked how I felt afterward, even if he didn't say anything back. This honesty opened up a whole new door for me. No matter how awful or sinful my thoughts or feelings were, I began to confess them to God and to myself.

Want to know a secret? I sucked at being promiscuous! It's true. I tried many times and I failed. I had plenty of numbers in my phone but the reality was I didn't call and I barely answered my phone. There were so many guys that would get a text from me and then never hear from me again or at least for months. I'd make plans but never go through with them. I'd even have some really good conversations but then I would disappear. Most of the guys in my contacts never saw me. They got sporadic conversations and nothing more would come from it. Whenever I did do anything, as I explained before, I would end up crying somewhere afterward. With that being said, my attempts at being promiscuous came to an end. I stayed close to Bryce.

I had a dream that scared the living daylights out of me. Maybe something within would have eventually given in to London again but this dream shut it down before it could ever happen. I dreamed that I was with London at some hotel and Bryce was trying to reach me but I kept ignoring his call. Then a giant white dove flew into the room and landed right at the foot of the bed. It gave me the sternest look I ever saw in my life and, considering I am terrified of birds, this dream was all it took for me to never consider giving in or going back to London and that dysfunctional lifestyle. We never spoke or saw each other ever again. London and I were finally over. A friend of mine would reveal that this dove was a representation of the Holy Spirit.

Because Bryce thought London was so crazy, he was relieved when he realized it was finally over. He wanted me to feel and be safe. We spent more and more time together and got closer, however, on a friendship level. We were not dating because we both felt we had a lot on our plates. Bryce prayed a lot and though he never would step foot in a church, he'd always encourage me to go. He talked to me about God quite often.

One night Bryce came over upset and frantic. He didn't want to talk about the issue at that moment but declared he needed some rest and my home was the only place he felt safe. I welcomed him in and I watched him sleep. I eventually fell asleep myself and I had another dream. This time it was about Bryce.

Yvonne Gurley

    I dreamed he was on a high-speed chase of some sort that lasted for days. I also saw him cut off his beautiful dreaded hair. In my dream, I saw him running from some men and while he was trying to run one of the men shot him in the back. The dream was so realistic, I woke up in tears. I became frantic though he remained sleeping.

    I felt helpless. I knew Bryce prayed a lot so I began to pray too. I no longer believed God or anyone could save me but I did believe God could save Bryce. It was now Bryce's turn to need protection.

My thoughts went everywhere and I couldn't have been more honest with myself or with God.

26 A Savoir

When your flaws are on the outside and obvious for the world to see, it is almost human nature to treat a person by the beauty that lies within. Contrary to this, when your flaws lie below the surface people don't try very hard to see you at all. You have to earn kindness and compassion. You have to prove yourself. I used to fantasize about being famous, that fame would finally allow me to be seen, but that's not true at all. I now know that fame would only put me in a larger room with a bigger crowd but I'd still be screaming for silence and still no one would hear me.

I didn't want to prove myself anymore. The next day, I decided not to give Bryce the details of my alarming dream. I simply told him I dreamed he cut his dreads. He laughed it off and stated he would never cut his hair. I also told him the part about him running from the men. He laughed that off as well. We wouldn't speak or see each other for a few months after this.

I returned to my path of self-discovery. I continued to make attempts to attend church but it was still very hard for me. I also continued to go out to night clubs with associates. Being in sin was so much easier than being saved, I thought. The club's congregation always welcomed you with open arms and no judgement.

Everyone was totally free to be who they were, whoever that might be. I battled with this for some time, especially Sunday mornings when I'd wake up feeling like the weight of the world was resting on my chest. If I made up my mind that Saturday I was going to attend service the next day, I'd have the battle of oppression waiting for me when I woke up. I literally felt chained to my bed. There would be such heaviness, and I felt powerless on those mornings. The dark clouds of depression lingered above my head on Sundays. I had no understanding of what I was battling; I just told myself that whatever it was I was no match for it, not alone anyway.

I didn't quite comprehend the order of the church and how it all worked. No one I personally associated with did either. In fact, my close circle was quite far removed. My sister and brother-in-law decided to give church a try as well and brought our uncle along with them to their place of worship. Uncle Joe was still pretty much under the influence from the night before. Somehow, he couldn't seem to find an "amen" or "hallelujah" to save his life. Instead, when he came into agreement with the pastor he yelled, "Hell yeah" and "You got damn right." Of course, everyone was appalled and my sister and her husband had to escort him out.

I was truly on my own in my journey of finding the Lord. I made up my own rules on how things should go.

Yvonne Gurley

I assumed that someone should be reaching out to me; surely someone had to notice my disappearing acts or sporadic attendance. I felt as though my inconsistency made me not counted among the numbers. Not a soul was aware I had gone away to Brightway. I just wanted someone to ask me where I had been. If just one soul would have inquired, I would have been so open to my troubles because I wanted relief. I could have shared the battles I faced on Sunday mornings and how not every Sunday I was the victor. Sometimes that heaviness got the best of me. Had they asked, someone could have been praying for me every Sunday because they'd know what I had to face and I'd no longer be fighting alone. No one ever asked me anything, and I had such high expectations for them too! Most people only hold the pastor to such high esteem but I felt it was the entire congregation's duty to care about everybody, even me. I mean, I had my friend from work but I considered her concern for me part of her friendship duties. I was back to feeling judged for my lack of consistent attendance and for being single, as most sermons addressed "the married people" in the room. I never thought such a small congregation could still leave room for one to feel so isolated and alone.

I had tried a larger church before and I felt like I didn't matter much there either. I saw the pastor and first lady out quite often and knew they had no clue that I attended their church at all. I was a stranger, just a number filling a seat. I thought getting away from that was my answer but it wasn't. Going somewhere smaller turned out to be worse because I wasn't hidden in the crowd anymore.

How could I attend a church so small yet still feel like I didn't matter? This truly baffled me. My growing hurt feelings were merely a distraction of the truth I had lost sight of. When I originally tried church, I was never looking for church but for a savior. I was desperate and never interested in much of anything else. Somehow, I lost that. I got caught up in feeling the need to prove myself for compassion. I didn't understand why the love wasn't free. Why couldn't I just show up and everybody love me just the way I was? They say, "come as you are," however, I felt there was a cavoite to that statement. I felt like they wanted to fix me first or have me fix myself and then come back. I wasn't on their level of worship and there was no time to bring me up to speed. Ultimately, I made the decision to disappear from the church again.

Late one night I got a random call from Bryce to come over. Since it was so late, I took offense to his phone call (I was taking offense to everything those days). I felt used by everyone, like I was swimming in the pool of charity. I was plagued by memories of London, replaying our relationship over and over in my mind and convincing myself we were never friends at all. I was the victim of a narcissist who sought me out like prey in my weakest moment just like Byron had done.

I felt guilty about my relationship with London and Byron for years after they were long gone. I also felt shame. Later in life it would be revealed that if I hadn't made all the mistakes, I made then it is quite possible I wouldn't be qualified for my purpose. Then I also thought that I'd rather be humbled by my flaws and mistakes then to have pursued a life of perfection and be one of those judgmental people whom never seem to gone through anything, never felt anything. Later I'd find I'd so much rather had been me, mistakes and all. My past affairs and addiction were my thorn in my side and allowed me to be filled with compassion before comparison or judgement of others sin. But that was much later, in that moment I felt so disposable. When Bryce contacted me out of the blue all I could think was "You want something too."

    I was rude. I felt disrespected and I made it my business for him to feel disrespected too. Realizing I may have overreacted, I contacted him and apologized for being so mean yet still explaining the cause for my reaction. I broke and told him how alone I felt. Before I knew it, he was at my door with the biggest smile on his face. He hugged me and told me I was crazy and we laughed it off. Bryce was the only person who didn't offend me when he called me crazy. We turned a comedy on and laughed until we could laugh no more. Suddenly, Bryce grabbed my hand. He looked me right in the eyes and said, "Yea you're crazy all right, but it's okay because I'm crazy too." He then shared how he hated crowds and how alone he felt as well. He talked about how nobody took him seriously about the demons he faced because of his appearance. The fact that women flocked to him no one around thought for one second that he battled with extreme anxiety or considered he was suffering at all. He explained having panic attacks in a room full of people yet no one ever noticed. After we both finished sharing, we decided he was me and I was him. We saw so much of ourselves in each other even more than ever before. We developed what seemed to be an unbreakable bond.

It would later turn out to be just another dysfunctional, co-dependent relationship. Bryce and I continued to talk sporadically but that was all about to change. My sister called me one evening, upset and told me I needed to come get my friend. I wondered who it could be because I didn't feel I really had friends. This friend turned out to be Bryce. He had gotten his dreads twisted at the salon where my sister worked. Well, he showed his tail that night. The salon manager threatened to call the police on Bryce because he pulled out a gun on one of the stylists. I pleaded with her not to call and immediately called Bryce. He was hysterical, screaming at the top of his lungs. I could barely understand him. I was afraid he might do something to get himself into trouble so I convinced him to come over where I knew I could keep him safe.

When Bryce showed up he was still screaming. I pulled him inside and just hugged him. I held him as tight as I could while he let it all out. I acknowledging the fact that he was screaming and paid attention to the words so I could begin to decipher what he was saying. I knew in that instant my dear friend had shown up to my door screaming "Silence!" and I was not going to ignore the obvious. He wasn't in the present moment but was yelling about something from his past. The things he yelled brought me to instant tears.

Yvonne Gurley

He screamed, "He pissed in my mouth. He threatened to beat me up. He threatened to kill me if I said a thing." I asked him who did that to him but he went on and on about his abuse without answering at first. After a while, he calmed down and told me about how he was sexually abused as a child as well as physically and emotionally abused. He talked about how no one saved him either. I asked him what happened at the salon to trigger all of his past hurt. He then proceeded to tell me the gay, male stylist had called him baby several times and gave the appearance to the other stylist that he was being flirtatious. This not only triggered Bryce's past but angered him because once again he found himself having to prove himself. He had warned the stylist but he wasn't taken seriously and it became a big joke to everyone in the salon as "the dread slayers" gayness was entertainment for everyone and he loved being the center of attention. Bryce had reached his boiling point on all jokes being on him and he snapped. He pulled the gun out on the stylist to show just how much he wasn't a joke. Of course, no one knew Bryce's story so his actions seemed unwarranted. But how could they have known? He wasn't just triggered, he was ignited!

This was all too familiar but not because of my own struggles, but it was very familiar as my sister found herself in this position as well at times. She was also the laughingstock in a crowded room. She was the psycho in other's world. She had a story too. She never talked about it, she never shared it with anyone but me. She told her secrets over and over again but who listens to the whispers when you can hear them clearly. People only lean in closer when it's not shared so loudly and boy did, she share out loud. Some say that most people end up crazy when they're older, after life has happened to them. She was already being called crazy when we were young. I like to think that my sister has never been crazy. Perhaps she had already found out then what we would all find out later. I know I did. Though we had different abusers, she and I would end up with similar fates.

Monsters do live under the bed and they really do hide in your closet just waiting for everyone to go to sleep. The world is so consumed, so well prepared for the thief who comes to steal your worldly possessions, but what about the thief who lingers, watching for the opportune time to steal your mind, your innocence, and sometimes even your soul?

When your flaws are on the outside and obvious for the world to see, it is almost human nature to treat a person by the beauty that lies within. Contrary to this, when your flaws lie below the surface people don't see you at all.

27 Awareness

My lack of wisdom was starting to become too expensive, yet, somehow, I continued to pay even though I knew I could no longer afford it. The enemy used the church to make it seem as though salvation was unaffordable. He made staying in sin seem uninhibited when in reality it cost a person the most valuable possession of all, one's soul.

When I wanted to pull away from it all I felt another pull and it was going in the opposite direction. I wanted God and the enemy wanted me. I was fighting for my life. My sinful world could see it, so everything one could think of was being thrown at me to make me feel more comfortable, safe enough to stay in it. Somehow it seemed as though the church could not see my fight at all. There were no efforts to get me to stay, only feelings of condemnation.

Bryce was arrested and had spent a few days in county jail. He had called me to let me know he was posting bond and how he wanted me to be there. When Bryce came through those doors he yelled out "friend" as soon as he saw my face. He picked me up and swung me around, giving me the biggest hug I ever had in my life. I could feel how happy he was to see me standing there and I was honored that my presence meant that much to him. We went out to my car and talked and then went our separate ways again. A few short weeks after, Bryce was back in jail and this time it would be for more than a few nights. He struggled to recover from the incident at the salon on the day he was triggered. His mind never recovered from it and he found trouble everywhere he went. I lost my friend. I would continue to talk to him from time to time but I'd lost him.

We were just coming off the holidays around this time. Nothing reminds a person who struggles with depression that their depressed quite like the holidays. My birthday, Christmas, and the new year had just gone by and I was trying to come up with a game plan for Valentine's Day. I wasn't about to let that holiday win too. I needed a break. I planned a trip with a friend and we escaped out of town. Was it the best trip I ever had? No, but it wasn't the worst. The trip went like everything went for me—fun at night and pain waiting to greet me bright and early in the morning, no matter what state I was in. The goal was to not sit at home alone feeling sorry for ourselves because it was yet another holiday rolling by to leave us feeling like we just got tissue paper rolled in our yards and eggs thrown. I know it's dramatic but that's the best way I can describe depression on a holiday.

I recall a coworker asking me how old I had turned when I was discussing my trip. When I told her she instantly frowned and said, "Yea, that's not a good time." I replied, "Wait, why did you say that? What isn't a good time? You mean turning twenty-seven?" She said, "Yes, turning that age or anything around that age is not a good time." I laughed but I was confused. She explained "because that's about the time you start to realize your life hasn't been going as planned and it isn't going to go as planned. It's when you find out you don't have anything you thought you'd have and you're not who you thought you were going to be. The feeling gets worse and worse as you get closer to thirty, so just hang on." I didn't know whether to laugh or freak out. *She was exactly right.* She later jokingly stated, "If your life sucks to you right now, just know that it's supposed to and everything is actually going according to plan." I was left with the "Wait, what?" face all afternoon after that and partially on the drive out of town. It didn't take much to send me into deep thought back then; shucks it still doesn't.

Anyway, we made it to our destination and there was a club attached to the hotel we stayed in. I had so much fun, I really did—I'm not going to lie. I wasn't thinking about anything or worried about anything for the first time in a long, long time. I believe it was the dancing. I loved to dance and I hadn't been dancing in quite a while.

Let me venture off my story and explain something about my depression before we continue. I know it may have come off like I was always sad and depressed but I didn't display that. I was fun. No, I was a really good time. My PTSD kept my depression lingering in the back of my mind, however, outwardly I was really fun to be around. I loved to laugh; I had an amazing sense of humor. I loved to party. The way my PTSD worked was depressive thoughts would spring up out of nowhere as if a trigger took place that I wasn't even aware of; even if I was having a good day, it would just send me into a really dark thought about my past. I'd have to have this mini fight in my head to shake it off. I didn't live in this constant mode of "I was abused as a child" but these jacked up thoughts and memories would pop up at random. Other than that, I was a fairly pleasant soul I'd say and others would agree. Perhaps I should have explained that much earlier but I think if there was a misunderstanding of me, getting an understanding now is actually the point of this journey because this was when I just starting to get an understanding of myself. I understand that the moments of joy I've shared thus far were accompanied with a level of irresponsibility and I've learned. But, even if there was a lesson behind it, I still appreciate every reason to smile I ever received. Every joke, every smile, every moment of bliss was medicine to my aching soul.

To jump right back where I left off—I hadn't danced in what seemed like forever, therefore, I danced my heart out. I probably looked like one of those people that you always assume doesn't get out much. Every song was my song that night, and I didn't care how I looked. For the moment, I was happy. As the partying came to an end, my friend and I decided to go ahead and walk back over to the hotel. Naturally after all that dancing, we worked up an appetite so we made the decision to grab a bite to eat before turning in to our rooms. I went to request the valet to bring my car around but it was very busy because half the club cleared out. My friend and I were kind of just lingering around, like others, waiting for the car and, you guessed it, there was this guy. Surely by now you all know no matter what there is always some guy that pops up.

    Anyway, this guy had been watching me but I was so hungry I began to kind of look around to see if I could locate the valet because we'd been waiting for a little while. As I'm looking, I walk pass the guy and he stops me and asks, "You looking for me?" I look back at him, kind of stunned, and the only thing I could think in my head was "uh-hm." So, to not look stupid, I quickly responded, "I don't think so." He responded, "Yea you are, you're looking for me." Now this guy was not a valet and didn't even work at the hotel but it was just his way of getting my attention. I admit it was a smooth move because he was able to start a conversation with me. He was very, very handsome. I mean, extremely handsome. I couldn't even believe this was happening because this was one of the few times I went out without intentions to find anything or anyone! It was Valentine's Day weekend and I didn't want anything to do with any guys at all. So, this guy hits me with his smooth line and we began to talk because he's making me laugh. By the time I finally got my car, he agreed to let us follow him and his friends to the restaurant. We continued to indulge in our conversation at the restaurant and then decided to exchange numbers and go our separate ways.

Nobody's Baby

The next day my friend and I were making plans for the day since we did not have a set schedule. Ultimately, we ended up doing what everyone does when they're out of town and don't know what to do—we went to the mall and grabbed something to eat. The charming man from the night before met us at the mall with his friend. They asked us about our plans for the evening but we still had no clue. His friend suggested we go to his job—at a club. We agreed to go.

This is where I'm sure you want to look at me like I'm outlandish, if you haven't already. I'm very much aware that one minute I'm spiritual and have moments with God and I'm dreaming and praying and trying to do the right thing, and the next minute I'm going in the opposite direction, but that's how it really was for me. I have to tell it like it really was. I can't tell you how many stories I've heard or read in which the person seemed perfect before taking his or her walk with Jesus, and those stories didn't help me. I could never see myself in anyone because it seemed like everyone was just so perfect, I did not want to bother with them. I didn't hear anyone's story about how they got caught in the trap of married men, fighting addiction, or looking for love. I didn't hear anyone talk about half of the things I've mentioned. I'm sure it's a lot of stories out there like it but let's just say the enemy made sure I didn't ever get to hear them. The enemy had me feeling extra alone and extra unqualified. This is how my walk truly went. I was trying to seek God and trying to pray to do right but you have to understand that Satan was working overtime on me. I had been walking on the wrong side for so many years, the enemy did not want to lose me. I couldn't see it because I didn't feel like I was that special for the enemy to even be bothered by what I was doing or not doing. It never crossed my mind that I mattered enough to have the enemy plan and plot things out in my life. By thinking like that, I never saw the attacks coming. I stayed blindsided because my spirit was never prepared. I was convinced I had no purpose or anything to contribute to the world and my life did not matter. I felt so unwanted at the church and so welcomed at the club.

This might seem obvious but at the time I wasn't thinking like that.

There would be times I'd just feel miserable and my first idea would not be to run to the church or even to pray. I was thinking more along the lines of "I'm going to go out because I feel like crap." I wanted to go where I felt loved and people would greet me with pleasantries and generally ask how I was doing or notice if I was not around the previous week. I couldn't figure out why I couldn't get this same greeting and love at church when I went. This was what I desired from church but could not get it and, in fact, I could barely get anyone to say anything to me at all when I went. On the other hand, going to the club involved greeters (technically they were ushers) who took time out to speak to me, even if for only a few minutes. Little things like that were magnified in my head, tricking me into thinking I was more loved and better cared for while living in sin. Accommodations were always made. The foolery was endless, people calling and checking on me if I hadn't gone out in a while wanting to see if I wanted to go out, offering to cover the cost, all to make sure I was going to keep going out and keep "having fun." Meanwhile, nobody called and checked on me from the church. If I hadn't been in attendance in a while you can just bring on the stares, the judgement, and the condemnation when I did attend.

I'm compelled to bring even more clarity to this situation. Everything I've shared about my experience with church is not intended to make church as a whole or the church I attended look bad. I actually don't think the church I attended was bad or the congregation or the pastor was mean. I do not believe that at all. I honestly think the enemy was just working on me and constructed an atmosphere to create chaos around me because he didn't want to lose me. Again, I was naïve to all of this because I felt like I wasn't that special. However, situations were certainly being crafted just to attack me.

My emotions were being manipulated. Remember how I stated that whatever you believe will find its way to prove to be true to you? Well, what did I believe? I believed I was unwanted, unloved, condemned, not good enough, and judged; this is all what I believed the church and its members felt about me. In turn, if the enemy was manipulating my emotions by transforming my beliefs into his own truths and lies, then why wouldn't he be doing this same thing with the pastor and the congregation, thus making what everyone believed about me to be what was true to them as well.

Oh, he certainly set up the scene. He kept people on my line calling, practically begging me to go out even if I had no plans to even go anywhere. He had these people offering to pay for everything just so I would venture into his atmosphere. None of this was obvious to me back then since I wasn't able to decipher Satan's moves against me.

Looking back, an awareness was needed because I'd get discernment but then the enemy would seem to overshadow it or block it somehow. I'd have times when I'd make a clear decision, like I didn't want to do something I didn't think I should date a certain person and I'd actually try to hold true to my decision. Then my emotions would be manipulated, my heart strings would get tugged, and before I knew it I was in another messed up situation again. Without fail, every time I thought I could trust my gut feeling this voice within, my discernment, would deceive me. I didn't know who to trust. I'd try questioning God like, "God, can I trust you because I thought I was hearing from you?" yet I couldn't decipher when I was hearing from God or when Satan was whispering.

Getting back to the trip, we did go to the strip club and I hated every minute of it. I couldn't wait for the night to be over. The next day was Sunday, Valentine's Day. That morning I got a call on the hotel phone from the front desk letting me know I had a guest waiting for me in the lobby. I was confused wondering who the heck was there for me. Then when I went downstairs Mr. Are-you-looking-forme was dressed in a full suit with flowers in his hand. I was shocked! When he handed the flowers to me with a smile, he asked, "Will you be my valentine?" I had never experienced anything like that before in my life. He knocked every romantic experience I ever thought I had right on out of the park with that move. He was just a real smooth dude, like out of a movie scene.

Even though this was a nice gesture, I couldn't feel it. My spirit would not allow me to be moved by too much of anything. My heart was cold and though he made a nice attempt, I didn't care because I couldn't feel. He was something new and I didn't have time for something or somebody new. I was amused but that was it. I went back to my room with the flowers in hand and, of course, my friend was wondering what the heck was going on and where the flowers came from. After I told her she gave me so much attitude! I got so much attitude from her that I shut down. Once more I was getting grief from a woman who didn't even realize I was too broken and too messed up to even take in what just happened. My day was completely ruined and we drove home.

That same day, I was surprised when I heard from Bryce. He was no longer in county jail but had been transferred to the state mental hospital. Bryce needed emotional support and reached out to me. Having my own experience in this type of facility, I wanted to make sure I was there for my friend. I really did go all out for Bryce. I wanted more than anything for him to be saved.

When he came home from the hospital, he clung to me for dear life. He prayed a lot; I had never saw anyone pray as much as him. He began to push me to give church a try again. He also wanted me to give sober living a try, as it was a condition of his probation. Bryce was a heavy marijuana smoker. Though I didn't go back to pills I smoked marijuana and drink way more than ever. But, with Bryce's insistence, I gave it all up. I cared about him so much and didn't want him to feel alone. It was hard dealing with Bryce because it also forced me to deal with myself.

I would complain to God a lot about Bryce and each time he'd always show me new ways to look at myself no matter how wrong I thought Bryce was. I used to think he was so selfish, but aren't we all? The broken ones get so wrapped up in trying to make the world see and feel our pain that we forget there are others out there just as broken as we are; we're still needed in this world. I made it all the way to twenty-seven and someone had yet to tell me that and I had yet to find it out for myself.

I took Bryce's advice and began to attend church again. It was like it always was with the same looks and stares. You know that feeling you get when you know someone was just talking about you before you walked up to the group? That was the feeling I had every time I went to church! I ignored it and pressed on. I had been in a great deal of heavy prayer; I will tell you that Bryce ran me straight to Jesus! He kept me on my knees night and day being so worried about him.

I was new to dealing with my problems from a spiritual aspect and felt I needed a little help. I reached out to the pastor whom advised he was leaving for a conference. I panicked. I really needed some answers as I felt something was coming; I didn't know what but I felt it. I reached out to another member of the church who was a musician. He was so helpful to my friend I thought he might give me some good advice as well. I didn't have his actual phone number, so I simply sent him my questions via Facebook messenger. After I got no response, the pastor passed me along to the first lady and I was able to ask her all of my questions. Not long after, the church musician also began to respond. I think I was so distracted and distraught that I didn't even catch the enemy at work. The musician responded to me inappropriately but I ignored his comments and redirected the conversation. The first lady had given me the answers I needed anyway so I moved on to focusing on her advice.

A few days later, I was out to lunch with my friend and another member from the church. I told them all about my questions and how the first lady helped guide me along. I also told them about the musician and his response. They advised me to report it to the pastor. I didn't know church politics so I just did what I was told. The pastor contacted me asking if I'd be willing to forward him the conversation from messenger. I did so, very willing because I felt I had nothing to hide. I'm certain there was a conversation between the pastor and the musician because after the report the musician kept giving me the stank eye, as if I did something wrong to him. A few months later the musician's wife sent me an email as if I had an affair with the musician. I was completely blindsided and pissed off. I ignored her lovely email as I refused to even have to defend myself or argue about it at all. She too started to stare at me at church and it took every ounce of my soul not to say anything to her, as I had nothing nice to say. I was fed up with everything. I had been trying to reach out to the pastor and the first lady but I was unsuccessful. I felt like no one had my back.

    I had already put distance between me and Bryce as he was growing to be too much. Though I created this distance, I still had a soft spot for him. The fact that I wanted him to be saved never changed no matter what he did. There was so much going on between things at the church and Bryce that I needed a distraction. I enrolled in real estate school to become an agent. Going after this filled me with so much joy. Not only that, but a friend suggested I give acting a try also.

    I had never done this in my life but she was so sure I should indulge even further into the arts. I auditioned for my first play and I loved it. With no training at all, I impressed my castmates with my ability to cry on cue. They all asked how I was able to do it and I thought to myself how just one thought about the reality of my life was worth shedding a tear over. Heck, I didn't even have to go back far in my life, I could just use my emotions from the day before. I would eventually go on to get some jobs as an extra in a movie being filmed locally. Participating in the movie assured me and gave me confirmation that acting, aside from writing, was my new love. During this time, I also went to tax school to get my license to prepare taxes. As you can see, when I say I distracted myself, I really distracted myself. However,

Nobody's Baby

my newfound joy from all of these things would be short lived.

It was my last week of real estate school and I was preparing for my exam. I was home studying when Bryce called. I had let him know that he had left his phone case at my house. He seemed to be in good spirits and mentioned he would come by to pick it up. By the time he come by, I had already picked my daughter up from school and we were having our normal after school chat about her day. There was only one point in my life when I ever thought a person to be possessed and that was my abuser as a child. Bryce was now the second person. He was at my door but it was not Bryce; when I opened the door, he was cursing and screaming at me, being very pushy and aggressive. He didn't hit me but I certainly felt like it was a possibility I was going to have to hit him. I instructed my daughter to go straight to her room and to not come out until I said. When I was able to get him out the door, I noticed he had a friend follow him in a separate vehicle; the friend looked just as possessed as Bryce. By the time we are outside of my tiny condo, I was very angry that Bryce would have such disrespectful behavior in front of my child. But then instead of getting in his car to leave, he grabbed a gun from his car and started threatening to shoot me. I was enraged and began to entice Bryce to do it. He rushed over to me and held me in place with one arm and put the gun to my head with the other. He was threatening to kill me but in that moment, with one tear streaming down my face, I told him to do it because I was tired anyway. I had no fear, no fear at all. When I told him to do it, in that moment I meant it. There was nothing duplicitous about me or that statement at the time.

He continued to hold the gun to my head and pushed the barrel harder and harder, attempting to bring about fear. The less fear I showed the angrier he became. It seemed as though this lasted for hours. My neighbors all ran outside to bear witness to the commotion. Out of nowhere, a wave of peace came over me. My anger felt like it had been zapped out of me. I began to tell Bryce I was going to pray for him and how much God loved him. As much as I wanted to die, I instantly wanted to live.

Bryce was so freaked out by my obvious change of spirit that he took off to his car with his gun in hand and drove off. I walked right back into my home and resumed making dinner with my daughter as if nothing ever happened.

One of my neighbors called the police so they came banging on my door. I was reluctant to tell them anything but since my neighbors had witnessed the entire incident made it quite difficult to deny the altercation. Additionally, the police were looking for him before he ever came to my house as his child's mother had already made accusations suggesting he might be at my house for a stunt he pulled with her. Needless to say, I was subpoenaed to court.

I recalled the night before how I had prayed Psalms ninety-one over my life. I truly believe it saved me. I kept feeling like something was coming but I didn't know what it was—until I opened the door for Bryce.

Nobody's Baby
It never crossed my mind that I mattered enough to have the enemy plan and plot things out in my life. By thinking like that, I never saw the attacks coming. I remained blindsided because my spirit was never prepared. I was convinced I had no purpose or anything to contribute to the world and my life did not matter.

28 Habits and Beliefs

Sometimes the cure is painful. So many cures we run from because we know it will be painful, or at least that's what we tell ourselves. We stay in the hurt that is familiar to us rather than introduce ourselves to a pain that is foreign to us even if that pain leads to peace. Isn't that something?

I know earlier I mentioned Byron got to me when I was extremely broken and weak and all of those things. While that may be true, one part of the truth was that Byron and I connected from misery. I was swirling in pain when I met him and I continued to swirl in pain the entire seven years I was with him. It was all I had to bring to the table and it was all he had, therefore, we produced what we had, which was misery. The other part of the truth was my obvious parental issues. My father was an addict with a mental illness and came in and out my life as he pleased. My father was also a survivor of childhood abuse and molestation. Every guy I dated was an addict with mental illness and made themselves as available to me as they pleased. My mother had an addiction to pills and dated nothing but married men. My mother was also a survivor of childhood abuse, rape, and molestation. So many generational curses waiting for me before I ever stepped foot into this world; my parents were never equipped to be parents at all. I started my adult love life with married men and ended up with my own addiction to pills. Everything I hated and judged my parents for I became. The irony! I wondered just like you're probably wondering; why is growth, healing, and maturity taking so long. Because it's taking my parents this long. As of today, even after my story is long over, they are still stuck.

Though I was no longer eighteen when I met London, I still had the mentality of an eighteen-year-old. London and I connected from fear of transition. We were both too proud to ever say it but it was indeed the vicissitudes of both our lives. We made each other feel safe to walk into the future because we used one another as some sort of safety blanket.

I hadn't grown at all after Byron. That entire seven years I was with him; I never matured. London was another guy who turned out to be nothing more than a mirage. It was detrimental that I learn to stop linking up with people with whom I could not grow from, could not learn from. The main problem was society—it doesn't care! Society doesn't care if you're going through something, if you don't know any better, if you're broken, or if you've been lied to! All everybody sees is the married part, the adultery part, the you-are-so-wrong part. The only way I was going to get out of what seemed to be a cycle was to not be weak, not be blind, and not be broken, or what some would say stupid. Those were all of my excuses for finding myself in bad relationships so the only way was to be the opposite of those things. I was not the woman who dated married men, I was not helplessly promiscuous. I was not an addict or any of the other horrible characteristics I had been displaying. Something inside me wanted to prove it.

Bryce and I connected from unfinished business, we were both running from ourselves. I had been avoiding the mirror and so had he. We were so busy running that we ran smack into each other. This forced us to see our reflections because when I looked at Bryce I saw myself. We didn't like each other because we didn't like ourselves. It was complicated, I know, but this complication was the glue that held us together. When I looked at him, I saw someone who was hard to love, difficult to understand, and more broken than words could describe, yet he was also so beautiful and well put together on the outside. Beautifully broken is what we were. I looked at him and saw someone who couldn't be trusted yet I wanted to tell him all my secrets. Bryce was me, he was so me.

I had the nerve to keep thinking why I kept running into the same type of people and blaming bad behavior on the other person. Not realizing if I was really running into the same type of people or just bringing the same person to every party hoping for a new experience. I proclaimed London to be a narcissist who came after me when I was weak, but looking back all I can say is I shouldn't have been weak. How much is it really any guy's fault for any "bad friendships" I feel I had? Is anyone at fault because there might have been some character flaws on their end, but the common denominator in all of those relationships was me.

At some point I had to have put my own "kick me" sign on my back. Up until then, I was blaming everything on everyone and I wanted people to feel my wrath. I wanted to make people understand because I didn't understand. I thought that maybe if I told you about me you could tell me about me because I don't know. When I left my mother's house, I was not certain of my identity or anything else one should be certain of at that point. What I was certain of was I couldn't trust myself, my judgement, or my gut feelings—I could not trust me at all. You see, the world had convinced young Stacey long ago that trust within herself was something she lacked.

I believe it was the silence. When I was young and vocalized my abuse or my feelings in general, I was always silenced and ignored. I was eventually convinced that my abuse never happened at all. It made me question every gut feeling I ever had after that. It also made me think that whenever I felt like I was being mistreated I was probably just overacting. From then on, people were always able to easily convince me their mistreatment of me was just in my head. A child being abused in any type of way knows that the abuse is wrong. It doesn't have to be taught or explained; some knowledge of injustices in life we get for free. It is the world that convince us otherwise and makes the abuse the natural feeling. I carried so much stuff inside of me, hardly ever letting anything out. My abuse showed up in my dreams, the trauma showed up in my PTSD, yet I had convinced myself that nothing ever happened to me at all. The secrets, the lies, the hurt, and the pain kept showing up in everything in my life and I didn't know how to deal with something that I told myself never happened.

    I blamed my parents or my lack of parents. I blamed my siblings. I blamed everybody. Maybe for some portion of my young life a lot of things were indeed their fault, but the minute I decided my life was up to me it stopped being anybody's fault but mine. I needed to deal with what I knew. I knew I lacked guidance, morals, selfrespect, self-worth, and self-love. I lacked so many things. Contrarily, how was an eighteen-year-old girl supposed to know she needed those things, especially if nobody told her? I knew I lacked those things but I didn't know until the damage had already been done and I had broken my own heart a million times. It got to a point where the blame and fault no longer mattered. You know what is my fault? Not seeking wisdom! The moment I realized and understood what I didn't have I should have sought out discipline, self-respect, and self-worth and then start to love myself. I should have pursued those things.

    I wasted so many years of my life being bitter because of all the things I didn't have. I was resentful because I wondered why nobody taught me. Why didn't I know any better? I kept reaping the repercussions of not knowing any better. However, it was always my responsibility to seek it out. I had it in me all along to knock on wisdom's door and say, "Teach me, show me what I don't know. Whatever I don't understand, make me understand."

I put way too much responsibility on other people. When I finally knocked on wisdom's door, wisdom answered! I probably became more aware than I was ready for. I didn't know it was going to come so fast. I received discernment more than I've ever felt in my life.
However, the enemy distracted me with my heart. He knew I was seeking wisdom. Satan knew he was about to lose me. He knew I was done with the church and seeking the one who saves, so he became frustrated. He threw everything at me that he could, like sending Bryce to hold a gun to my head. You know what though—I fought back! Not right away, but eventually I'd make the decision to fight back!

At that point in my life, I felt like I had been running non-stop and I was about to jump off a cliff. I wasn't jumping to die; I was jumping to live! I just knew when I jumped that my father in heaven indeed was going to save me. You see this scenario in movies sometimes when someone has done all they can to keep their enemy away until they get to the edge of that cliff and there are no more options so they look at the ledge and then look back at their opponent. This was where I was, right in that moment when I was running and thinking if I stayed where I was and let the enemy have his way with me, I would surely die, but if I jumped I just might make it. Even if I didn't make it, at least I tried and didn't just allow the enemy to take me.

Nobody's Baby

Life hurt. I hurt. Even though I had so much anger toward Byron, it did hurt me to leave him. It also hurt me to walk away from London. I was going through so much hurt. My friends, the ones I thought were friends, were falling off left and right and that hurt me. Church hurt me too, but like I said sometimes the cure is painful. I thought I went into this thing with Bryce with my eyes wide open but there were so many things I was missing. I thought Bryce was another attempt for me to continue to ignore myself, another distraction for me to use; however, he turned out to be my Nineveh and I was Jonah. Having compassion for Bryce, learning to love and forgive him allowed me to do all of these things for myself because I stopped ignoring me and started seeing myself. Every time I complained to God about Bryce I was really complaining about me. In hindsight, it makes so much sense why God kept dealing with me whenever I'd complain.

Sometimes we can get so caught up in wanting to save others that when the other person decides to fall on his own sword we forget that we were standing right behind him, connected to him. When that person hurts himself, he hurt us too. It would later be revealed to me that Bryce had more going on than I could have imagined and I didn't begin to have the power to save him. Though my relationship with Bryce put me through a lot, I learned so much about myself—after the fact. I wish I had learned you can't save people in my teenage years but, unfortunately, I had to take that hard lesson in my twenties—I had to have my life threatened before I learned it.

Part of my problem had a ton to do with what I believed about myself. I thought I was so jacked up that I had to date people who were just as jacked up as me or worse. I told myself a "normal" person would never understand. I got caught up in this lie when I left Byron. Because he never experienced any type of trauma, I found myself on trial almost daily between him and his family. It was a lot of "Why does she act that way?" or "Why does she look like that?" type of thing. After enduring seven years of trials for my personality, I was done dating people who never endured anything.

Speaking of my feelings about trials, I struggled to be a part of Bryce's trial. Every part of me did not want to go to court. I did not want to be a part of his judgement. On one hand, I wanted there to finally be a consequence to someone hurting me, but on the other hand how could I state what I feel someone deserves when I've hurt people and I've threatened people too? The only difference being I was never punished. In my younger days I had hit someone with my car—on purpose. I had also held a knife to someone's throat and on more than one occasion because my anger and PTSD used to be that bad. I couldn't take feeling emotions without exploding. Heck not too long before that incident I threatened London with a hammer; what if he had called the cops on me? I felt like I was in no position to take part in someone else's condemnation. I prayed more than I ever prayed in my life, distracting myself from my own wounded feelings with the protection I felt Bryce needed. The court date kept getting pushed back and I didn't want to live out that day anymore. I made the decision not to cooperate. The State had picked up the case anyway so he was getting charged whether I witnessed it or not. I just wanted it to be over so I could move on with my life.

I was quite numb after that. The numbness is why I allowed Bryce to stay in my life. I should have given myself permission to feel the pain from it all but I didn't. I had mistaken my numbness for forgiveness and I let him stay in my life a whole extra year, but I didn't forgive him and I didn't forgive myself. I was struggling mentally and emotionally. This was all too much. I thought I was fine but I wasn't.

I thought I needed my parents so much. My therapist, Dr. Yola would always try to get me to let them go and accept they would never be who or what I needed or wanted them to be. Accepting this felt like I was mourning someone who was not dead. Every time I came in contact with my mother, I had to have a mini funeral in my head for her and I was exhausted of going to her funeral. It was the same way with my father. Yes, at the beautiful age of twenty-eight he decided I existed to him again. I hadn't been in contact with him since I was eighteen. I was still just as hurt and angry and the fact that he's schizophrenic couldn't change how I felt about his abandonment. That wound dug a hole so deep that being in my life for just a few years wouldn't heal it. Though he tried, there was a level of trust that could not be restored. In the back of my mind, I was still leaving space for him to leave again, so I only allowed him to get so close.

I used to joke all the time and say the only thing left to happen to me was for a lion to eat me alive, or a random elephant trample through my house, or a piano fall on my head. I mean, I really felt like I had gone through everything. What Bryce had done felt like he simply tossed a bucket of water over my head. My mind, heart, and spirit had no more room for any more trauma to be experienced. I felt like Job, Jonah, and David from the *Bible*, all at the same time. First of all, I felt like Job because of all the things that happened that I didn't bring upon myself or ask for but somehow I suffered with no one to give me an explanation as to why; Jonah because I spent a lot of time running from God and what he wanted me to do and blaming other people in the process; and lastly, David because I continued to find myself in the kind of trouble that only God could save me from.

During the trial, I did have one final attempt to reach out to the church but nothing ever came of it and I was ignored. It was the final straw for me. I could not understand why it was so hard to be acknowledged when there were so few members. I wasn't asking for special treatment. I watched how supportive and involved they were with others but I couldn't even get a courtesy call. I was told my messages were never received—a convenient excuse. I took it so hard because I felt like the church ignoring me was akin to the ignorance I received from my family, my friends, and God! I exploded. After I realized I wasn't going to get a response I sent another message, not asking for prayer or guidance but expressing myself with no reservations. And just like the Devil, you better believe they got that message. I went on to explain in full detail how I felt my entire experience being a part of the church or my lack of it. At the time, I felt like the only one who tried to acknowledge me was my co-worker who was also member. She became my friend because her treatment of me was a perfect example of a witness. No matter how much I did or didn't show up, she always treated me with gentleness, kindness, and respect. When I went to her about anything, she always tried her best to show me where God was and convince me not to give up. I thought very highly of her and I let it be known that, in my opinion, she was a stellar example, no matter how great everyone else thought they were.

However, this backfired in a way. The church took it as though she had betrayed them because I had mentioned her so much. Somehow my feelings and my actions were her fault. Because she loved the church and the congregation so much, she was pretty much forced to choose without anyone having to say it. I always felt it though we tried to hang on to our friendship after this, but it would never be the same.

I shut down. I felt nothing. For an entire year I felt nothing! I couldn't feel. Even when I wanted to, I couldn't feel. I had no church to run to, no friends to run to, no drugs, no nothing. Again, I threw myself into heavy prayer. All I had was God and he was about to show me that having just Him was exactly what I needed, and He was more than enough.

Yvonne Gurley

We run from so many cures because we know it will be painful, or at least that's what we tell ourselves. We become familiar with one pain rather than introduce ourselves to another unknown pain, even if that pain leads to peace.

29 Lies

I dreamed that I drove to a previous address and when I walked in it was as if time had been frozen; either that or everyone just bailed. While walking around, I was complaining about the mess and before I knew it the walls began to crack. As the walls were cracking, I began to scramble trying to find my keys before the house caved in on me and just before I found them, I woke up. I had no idea what that dream meant but it was so real. I tried to find any interpretation I could online but I was unsuccessful. The internet gave me too many options and, as an indecisive person, this did nothing but frustrate me. So, I prayed and asked God to please show me what it was he was trying to tell me because I did not understand.

Ask and you shall receive people! Little did I know the next time I went to sleep I had the exact same dream only this time God was with me. We walked through my old house together as he pointed to different items, asking me what the things represented to me. Each time I answered He always replied, "Let it go." Finally, when we got to the topic of my keys, I noticed God was holding my missing keys in his hand. He asked me, "If you lost your keys today, would you think to go to a previous address to find them?" Of course, I replied no. In response, He asked,

"Then why are you doing this with your life?"

Talk about an "ah-ha" moment! I had been so busy digging in my past, focusing and complaining about everything that's ever happened to me, that when it was time to go to my future I couldn't find my dang keys!

For the longest time I floated in the middle—afraid of making the mistake of being who I once was but also afraid of who I was to become. I called it playing it safe. I actually lived my life and made most of my choices based upon something being better than nothing; not realizing that saying is just a suggestion of being humble and not foolish. In fact, sometimes nothing is better than something and other times you deserve more than just something.

Validation was a big problem for me. I learned that I don't like what it feels like for my voice to not be heard, especially when I'm speaking so loudly. At times I felt I had not given my all—in school, in my relationships, or to myself. But most importantly, I refused to give my all to God because I was so afraid of disappointments and not being validated for my good efforts. Yet I expected to receive the benefits of someone who had truly done her best.

In my relationships, I refused to love anyone all the way and if you loved me, well, that was at your own risk.

I found out that I don't like pain and the only thing I didn't like more than pain was new, unrecognizable pain. I was comfortable with hurt feelings in areas I had already felt; those pains were so devastating to me that I refused to take the risk of a new pain in a new spot hurting me even more than the last one. What I got from guarding my heart and my life from new pain was exactly that—the same pain, mistakes, and life lessons happening over and over again. Being guarded not only kept the new pain out but it also kept out new peace, new joys, and new happiness. I learned that I had to be willing to take the risk; however, not only did I have to take the risk but I also had to give everything my all. Luke 12:48 states, "To whom much is given, much is required."

The first thing I needed to do was identify all the lies in my life and the second was to stop believing them! Lies! Oh, how I bought so many lies. I believe the first lie was that I was alone and that I had to do life all alone. I did all of my suffering alone for majority of my life and I called it "being private." How foolish was I? From the very beginning, God looked at Adam and said, "It is not good for man to be alone." Even Jesus had disciples so why on Earth did I think I could handle life all by myself and never need anybody, even God?

I went through the phase of thinking I didn't need friends, family, or anybody. However, these were all just lies and excuses to keep people away from me because I was afraid to trust them for fear of being hurt. I needed help, but I wouldn't ask for any.

Aside from my mental health issues, being a single mother did its fair share of taking a toll on me as well. As a working single mother, I could never get any assistance when, and if, I fell on hard times. I was always told I made too much money because I only had one kid. My coworkers and I spent many days complaining how we saw mothers on assistance with their hair and nails done and always driving the newest cars while we scraped every dime we had just to make ends meet. Just dreaming of being able to buy yourself anything was out of the question. I always told myself if I ever got wealthy, I'd create something for working single parents so that they didn't have to go into credit card debt when life hit them. The difference it would have made if some months just one bill was paid for me. Overdraft protection and credit cards was all I knew because, again, I believed the lie that I was all alone.

For many years, just like my mother, I was emotionally unavailable to my daughter at the beginning of her life because I was drowning in the pain of my life. For so long, pills, partying, and men were what I thought I needed to get by.

I remember lying in bed just crying and speaking out loud about how tired I was and then out of the blue my boyfriend from high school, the Puerto Rican, reached out to me. He was coming to town and wanted to see me, as we always remained in a good space over the years. I hadn't been in contact with him for a little while but when he came it was as if God sent me an angel. He cooked dinner for my daughter and me, he helped with laundry—he did everything I never got a break from. I was able to go to work and come home without the entire world feeling like it was on my shoulders. He helped with my daughter's homework and played with her. I was so relieved to finally have some days when dinner wasn't up to me physically and financially. He even did my yard and I was just about to hire someone, which I really couldn't afford to do but I had no time for anything. He tried to remain in my life and even suggested us possibly getting back together but I was way too broken. In my mind, all of his good deeds would one day have to be paid back because every guy that entered my life started out being very good to me and in the end I paid for it. I didn't feel like going through anything at the time. Though I was very close to him, even when we were in high school, I never told him about anything I had gone through so when I acted out with him, I'm sure he thought I was just mean or crazy. Either way I didn't want him to see me as someone he had to rescue so I never told him. I made excuses and ran as far away from him as I could and I gave him no explanation as to why because I was convinced I didn't deserve anyone to be that good to me without me eventually having to pay for it later. To this day he does not know why I cut off communication or how much what he did meant the world to me. At the time I'd rather him believe I was just this unappreciative woman who took his kindness for weakness than to take the risk of being vulnerable and letting someone get close to me again. I never told him just how much I appreciated all he had done but I hope someplace deep within his heart he knows.

Now this next lie is a good one. Boy, this lie will have you bitter for a long time. The enemy can be so annoying, always trying to show and prove that God isn't enough or what you have in your life isn't enough. For example, if you're single, he shows you couples. If you have someone, he shows you happy single people. If you're lonely, there'll be people sharing and spending time with family and friends. If you say you're tired he'll even have someone pop up early in the morning with tons of energy. I mean Satan is the king of petty, okay! I told God, "No wonder you kicked him out, he's too petty!" Let me tell y'all how he was messing with me.

When I entered the ministry of singleness (and boy did being single minister to me but that's like a whole other book), if I went anywhere, like the grocery store, the enemy showed me happy couples and families everywhere. You see, he added the families in there too because I had been wanting another child, I just couldn't have another one with any of the people I dated. I mean come on, y'all read this book so you know I couldn't have kids with any of those men. The devil was messing with me so much in this area. It started to become obvious what he was trying to do and I got to the point I started laughing every time I saw one of his manipulations.

Another lie was God was like man! Whenever I didn't want to deal with a certain area of my life or even parts of myself, I assumed that God didn't want to either. I thought he was looking down on me and seeing me and saying to himself, "Oh no, I'm not fooling with Stacey today." I thought God felt like I was one of those people folks considered "doing too much." I had made such a mess of my life and I that I thought even the Lord didn't want to deal with me. That's the lie I believed. I mean I would pray my little heart out and get nothing in return. It got to the point where I thought heaven had a reject button or something because my prayers were not getting through to the man upstairs. Then I would pray some more, yet again nothing. So, then I thought my name was programmed under "Do not answer" because I was starting to think the prayer phone wasn't even ringing when I called. Jesus had me on blocked call, I just knew he did. After doing so much prayer and not being answered, I believed my only purpose or assignment in life was to suffer.

I thought negatively for so long with this concept that I even came up with a name for it because I'm that dramatic. Everyone has heard of the "Haves and the Have-Nots." Well, in my world there were the "Sufferers and the Good Lives." I assumed I was supposed to be a sufferer. The enemy had me convinced with these two lies that intertwined with one another—it's just you and everybody but you. Let me put this in perspective. Every time I would ask God for something, the enemy would show me everybody but me getting the very thing I had just asked God for. When I say I could not escape this I mean it. I could get on the internet, get on social media. I could just run to the store or out to eat and what do I get to witness but my prayer coming true for someone else!

The very thing I had been asking the Lord for was showing up right in front of me only somebody else was getting it. I'd think to myself, "See, I knew I was a sufferer." Lies!

I'd like to call the year I turned twenty-nine my "wonder" year. It was the first time in a while I wondered what if I tried a new church, what if I actually did have a purpose, what if love was something totally different from what I've ever experienced? What if I was stronger, more talented, and more beautiful than I ever believed? What if God was not how I thought he was and what if prayer didn't work the way I thought it did?"

Up until that point I had bought the lies, sold the lies, told the lies, and accepted the lies. I was so sick of all the lies in my life that by the time I turned thirty I wanted nothing but the truth. I was done lying to myself and letting others lie to me, too. I took so long to do better partially because I was afraid I was going to find out I was not as great as I thought. I didn't want all those negative voices I always heard to be right about me. This was a major role in why I was stuck for so many years. I'd rather stay not knowing my potential than to take the risk of finding out God or the enemy was right. Either way I didn't want to know. I had to stop thinking that nothing would work out for me and take into consideration that maybe it was not that nothing worked out but that God had a better plan for my life and things were going according to His plan.

I'm convinced God listens to our thoughts, indeed. I went to the park on my lunch break the next day, to stare at the river flowing. For some reason I think so clearly there. I normally don't get out of my car; I just drive up, park, pray, and think. That day was different. For the first time, I got out of my car. I took a few steps to see what spot would give me the best view and then I saw him! He was sitting on the only bench that was near. It took me a while to make my way over, as I can be shy at times; however, something just pulled me to him. I walked up and asked if I could join him for which he replied, "Sure."

He was much older; I always get excited around anyone older as I never experienced grandparents. He had binoculars hanging from his neck so I asked if he saw anything interesting and he said, "No, not yet. Not anything special anyways; just your average birds you see all the time." Right after he said that three birds that appeared to be doves came flying by in the distance. The man couldn't see any better than me and stated, "Well, I believe they are doves, either that or geese." We giggled! He began to tell me about a bird he didn't see anymore and how he missed it. We both wondered why it seemed they don't come around anymore but he explained, "As you get older, you'll miss a lot of things. You get used to it." He began to position himself as if he were going to leave and a small panic inside me burst out. "WAIT! I needed; I mean I wanted to ask you something." He smiled and said, "Well what's that?" I looked him in the eye and asked, "Is there anything in life that you get now that you wished you had sooner?" He smiled even harder as if he never thought I'd ask. Then he explained, "The first and probably the biggest thing is that you can't do life by yourself.

Don't even try and don't wait until you're old to figure that out. Learn and accept it now because it makes life a little easier the sooner you learn that one. You need something, someone higher than yourself to get through. By the way, are you getting all that you need spiritually? I hope you are and if you're not, try. Learn what's important now and base your living according to that. We take so much for granted. Oh yea, you should walk more. Take walks often. It's good for you. You'll find that out when you're old, too. Be careful with your chances. I took a lot of chances when I was young. After some of those chances, I shouldn't even be here. Well, I'd say that's about it." As he proceeded to get up again to walk away, he stopped and turned to me one last time and said, "You're gonna be fine, you know. You're going to get everything you want out of life. You're capable to do anything. You'll be fine, but remember to feed yourself spiritually."

That was it and then he turned back around and continued his walk and bird watching. I stayed on that bench a little while longer than expected in even deeper thought than before. As I got ready to leave, I realized we never introduced ourselves. I was sitting on that bench wishing I learned his name. Then his friend walked up and yelled to him, "Grover, hey Grover." I was so happy to know this. I got in my car and as I was driving away, Grover looked up and waved goodbye. His name was GROVER!

Yvonne Gurley

"If you lost your keys today, would you think to go to a previous address to find them?" Of course, I replied no. In response, He asked, "Then why are you doing this with your life?"

30 Truth

I have to admit I was terrified of turning twenty-nine. Can you blame me? Look at what every year had brought me thus far! It got to the point I was asking Jesus, "This whole turning twenty-nine thing, can we just skip it? Will you fast-forward me right to my thirties and just write a letter to let me know what happened for twenty-nine?" I did not want to go through anything else. Everyone kept telling me my thirties would be better, and I believed them. I clung to the hope of my thirties. I had finally hit that tired mark. You ever get so tired that you finally start thinking different? I mean, I was so tired by this point my entire concept of life changed. I even began to think differently about myself. I would find myself sitting up wondering about some of everything.

My wonder year of twenty-nine raised even more questions. I think I've always had questions but they were never the right ones. Now my questions were ones only the Lord could answer. Remember, I was trying to go about life alone, so who was going to answer my questions? I felt like God wasn't answering me so I told myself, "Jesus may not be talking to you but He is talking to somebody;" therefore, I had to go to church. So, I went!

Now I did not go to the same church. Even though I had my first experience of the "infamous church hurt" I viewed church just like I viewed buying something to eat: If one restaurant doesn't serve my favorite food the way I like, I'm not going stop eating or liking my favorite food. No, I'm going to just pick another restaurant that has a chef and customer service that serves me the way I feel best suits my taste. It was that simple. My church hurt was over. I saw where the enemy worked in my past church experience and moved on. The spirit of offense had been at work as the last two churches I tried I found myself offended in one way or another. I applied my theory to church as I did to my bad relationships. Once again, I was bringing the same person to the party expecting a new experience. I realized that if I wanted church to work, regardless of the function of the church, there was something in me or about me that obviously needed to change.

The new church was a couple of blocks from where I lived, which helped with my tardiness. It also helped with being absent because there weren't too many places I could go when I left my house without having to pass this church. They also had three different service times so I wasn't going to have an excuse for missing these services unless I was pretty much dying. It was a completely different experience, not just from my previous church but any church I had ever gone to. I've been attending there for a few years now and I can't tell you a single service in which I made it from my car to my seat without someone acknowledging my presence. No matter how many members I saw, they had made it a point to get to know me. It was the perfect demonstration of the one who leaves the ninety-nine for the one who's left behind. The Father knew what I needed and he knew just where to send me.

By getting to know me, they encouraged me to serve as they did all members. I had never served in church a day in my life. I was afraid of the commitment. I shied away from wanting to serve because I didn't want to pledge to be at church other than Sunday. This was my first reason for staying away. The other reason was I always felt like I wasn't good enough to serve. It had crossed my mind at my previous church and when I mentioned my interest I was told, "Let me pray about it first," but no one ever got back to me. I took that as confirmation that I needed a certain level of holiness to be a servant. That was another one of the devil's lies I fell for. The truth was God wanted me, loved me, and accepted me just the way I was and he demonstrated this through the way I was treated by his children in the new church. I was able to volunteer where my heart able to help the most—in the arts. I became a part of the media or creative team. My love for writing, acting, and the stage was once again awakened. I never thought in a million years I could serve God this way. I always thought it was a "your talent versus God" type of thing and you had to choose. The more I served the more my confidence grew. I began to even mentor other women in small groups as I figured I had mastered plenty of the what-not-to-do, the don'tgoin-there, and the what's-behind-door-number categories.

Even though my confidence was growing, I still wasn't quite there yet. I had reached a place where I had hope for everyone but me. Week after week, I witnessed so much life change but I was blind to my own story. It wasn't until I was asked to participate in speaking during an event for the women at church that I realized exactly where God was in my life and where I had it all wrong. I know this sounds strange, but I realized I had been approaching the Father like he was a famous person I wanted a selfie with when I would pray. To elaborate, if you've ever been in the presence of a celebrity you really want a selfie with them. It's like your trophy you get to display to the world or your proof of your "good experience." Up until that point, I didn't feel like I had any trophies, or selfies, with Jesus. I felt like I heard about him but I didn't have proof of him and I felt like everybody had gotten to take a selfie with him but me.

Needless to say, I was going to God but like I just wanted a selfie. You see, when you approach celebrities normally you don't introduce yourself or tell them your name or anything about you at all; you just go up to them and ask them for a picture and then you just walk away. After walking away, it never dawns on a person they just took a picture with someone and didn't even tell them their name. I had to realize that was how I was approaching God. I was asking him for things but I was never telling him my name. I had no interest in telling him my name or anything else about me and I wasn't asking him anything about him either. I was good with what I thought I read, understood, and/or heard about him. I never asked him personally what he was like or tried to tell him more about what I was like. I just saw it as he's God so he sees everything, thus, I don't have to have conversations with him or get to know him. Why would he want to get to know me? I mean he's famous, right? He didn't need to know my name. But those were all lies because the truth is a conversation is worth way more than the picture. I wanted to have this experience and I wanted proof of the experience so I could walk around saying I was blessed but I didn't want the relationship.

The reality was God wanted to mature me. He wanted me to get to know Him. The only reason I could never see where He was in my life was because I didn't know Him personally. I didn't know His ways or how He moved. I based how the Lord would treat me on how I thought He treated others. I mean, I was really wondering when this burning bush was going to show up and waiting for angels to appear. I just knew I was going to see Jesus walking on water or something. I didn't know how to see Him in my life or where he had been all along because He didn't look like what I expected so I assumed He was never there. Since He wasn't answering my prayers in the ways I thought they should be answered, I felt like I wasn't receiving anything from Him at all. The truth was I just couldn't recognize Him. When the disciples were in a storm, they couldn't recognize Jesus walking on the water, not at first because of their own views of Him, what they believed, and how they thought He should react. If they had based their expectation on how they knew Him personally, I believe they would have recognized Him immediately. Just like the disciples didn't, neither did I. My entire life thus far had been focused solely on the fact that I was in a storm no one, not God or anybody, was around. In reality, God was always there, I just couldn't recognize Him.

In all my experiences with the church throughout my entire life, I was continuously taught the discipline of God. I was taught to strive for this unobtainable perfection, to please Him. I had understood that I better let God love me or else. The problem with allowing the Lord to love me was that my idea of love was full of abuse and torture. I didn't have a good perception of love; therefore it was impossible to have a good perception of him because God is love, right? This was why I expected to be mistreated by Him and why I thought He assigned me to be nothing more than a sufferer in this world. I was never taught to strive to love God back. Oh, how life changes when you love Him back! I mean really love him back because when you love someone, your desire to do right by that person comes naturally. It's no longer forced or a task you feel you have to do. Everything you do from then on will be out of pure love and willingness. When I began to open up, to be completely vulnerable with God and treat him like He was really someone I wanted to get to know and love for real, everything changed. I finally told God my name.

Nobody's Baby

I told God all about me. I talked to Him like He hadn't witnessed a thing in my life. I shared all of my secrets and true feelings. He really became the best friend I thought I never had. I told him everything. There were times when I couldn't wait to be alone with Him so I could tell Him something. When I found myself feeling lonely, He was the first contact for me. We went on dates and I'd invite Him to watch movies with me. I even told Him jokes. God truly became my everything. I had forgotten all about Bryce and everyone else I dated. My relationship with Jesus brought me more comfort than I could have ever imagined.

Did my life all of a sudden become perfect? No! In fact, I found myself asking the Lord, "What is this?" more times than I can count. The development of my relationship with Jesus gave me permission to feel and have the confidence to trust myself. If I felt like I was being mistreated in any kind of way, I let myself feel it. I stopped running from it. I allowed myself to feel it and if I needed to question it, I questioned, but this time I didn't let the other person answer or confirm my hurt feelings. Instead, I made room for my hurt feelings, I felt it, then I brought it to God and by him, I was able to move forward. I would still give the other person a chance to acknowledge my hurt feelings, but my life no longer depended on that acknowledgment because God had already acknowledged it for me. If my hurt feelings were inaccurate, He would show me. If the person was indeed wrong or even if I was wrong, that would be revealed to me, too. No matter how the chips would fall when it came to my feelings, God acknowledged them and each time His acknowledgment would mature me so I wasn't as needy anymore.

Remember how I stated the truth was always visiting me, dangling its keys, but I tried to suppress these visits with pills and everything else? Remember the dream I had in which God was holding the keys to my life? Well, hello John 14:6: "I am the way, the truth, and the life. No one comes to the Father except through me." I had been trying to get through life avoiding the truth, avoiding wisdom, and avoiding getting to know Jesus and wondered why I felt like God wasn't there. When I told Jesus all about me, He began to not only show me things about Him, but He also showed me things about myself that He knew and I didn't.

For starters, I needed to conquer the spirit of loneliness because previously I always thought if I surrounded myself with people then I wouldn't feel lonely. I'd hang out with friends, yet still, feel alone. I'd go to church, yet still, feel alone. Then I'd think I just needed to be in a relationship, but after I had one, I still felt alone! No matter if it was one-on-one or in a room full of people, I kept finding myself feeling alone until Jesus revealed to me one day that the feeling of loneliness doesn't have as much to do with the company of others as I thought. I opened my eyes and began to really see what He was talking about. When I did finally get the time spent, the validation, the attention, and the love I always wanted, it still wasn't enough for some reason. I began to listen to Him, to believe Him. Once I realized it for myself, I questioned what feeling lonely was really about because I was constantly around other people and felt like they understood me, yet I was still experiencing the same feeling. The answer came in one word—wholeness! I felt lonely because I wasn't whole! With that being discovered, I shifted my focus from bonding with others to bonding with myself and with God more. I ended up having to deal with this in stages.

In my past, I feared lonely so much that I'd do almost anything to not feel it. I'd hang with people I had no business hanging with—people who didn't truly like me as a person and to be honest I didn't like them either. I thought regardless of the dynamics I was beating feeling alone. I was staying in unhealthy relationships just trying to remain one step ahead of being lonely, but in reality, I was never ahead of anything other than ignorance. I would say I compromised my morals and values but I was so afraid of being lonely that I didn't have any. I definitely had to get those.

I was determined to beat lonely because I was tired of lonely making a mockery out of me, teasing me, letting me know he was still there after I had done something that was morally wrong only to make me feel like I was getting what I deserved after all of my actions. So, I began to live my life and treat myself differently and so much better that lonely had nothing to prove to me anymore. There was nothing he could through up in my face or tease me about. I was taking away his power because I was no longer running from myself or my past. I actually began to not just like myself but love myself and I made no apologies for it. I stopped freaking out when I knew relationships needed to come to an end. I no longer felt like if a person went away I didn't have anybody. I became confident and bold. I knew no matter what I had myself and I had Jesus and at the end and beginning of the day that would always be enough. It's not that I developed the I-don't-need-anybody mentality, I just was confident that no matter what I had somebody, even if that somebody was just me or just God.

I learned it was okay to feel like that if it was for the right reasons. I got an understanding that it was okay to desire a lot of things too, like a better life, a husband, and a career, as long as my reasons were coming from a good place. Ultimately, the world made me feel like I was selfish for wanting anything and then church culture made me feel worldly if I wanted anything at all, which resulted in feeling like I didn't deserve or should want nothing. The issue I was having was though both of these are partially true, it's not true in the way I was making myself feel about it all. It all boiled down to checking my reasons. What was my motive behind everything? I was handling everything else the way I had handled prayer: I was praying because I wanted a blessing not because I wanted to know God. Through getting to know the real me, I realized everything I wanted was for worldly reasons. I wanted things for the appearance of my proof of me living a "good life." I wanted a husband and lots of friends because I wanted to prove somebody picked me. I had a few other reasons but that was the main one. It was because society treats females like we're lower if we're not in a relationship or have tons of female friends; therefore, I was always striving to prove I was worthy. One day I sat down and made a list for why I wanted a husband and every single reason was worldly. I couldn't believe that truth about myself.

You see, God doesn't just expose the truth to you about others, he exposes the truth to you about yourself and that's something I had to put my grown-up pants on to see. A person that wants a partner for worldly reasons is always going to be a selfish partner. I saw that if I had been given a husband my marriage would be as fickle as my reasons for wanting one. Nothing would ever be good enough and if it was good enough it wouldn't be for very long because the world is always changing and evolving. The entire world is capricious so I couldn't possibly base what I wanted from what I see on TV, the internet, or in other people. I had to change my reasons for everything I wanted or else I wasn't going to get very far and everything I gained would always be temporary and, eventually, meaningless.

I used to be so consumed with the fate of everything that caused me to struggle with faith and have anxiety. I thought when I hopped in the pool with Jesus, I was just going to grab my floaty and drift along the lazy river of life. Obviously, that's not what happened. I jumped in the pool, lost my float a couple of times, and ultimately realized life with God was nothing like a lazy river but more like a wave pool. Even though I had a floaty, my experience would be less scary if I also knew how to swim. I had lots of swimming lessons and learned from them all.

My wonder year of twenty-nine, which I feared so much, ended up being one of the best years of my life, so far. I took trips, I studied, I served in the church, and God even let me be a part of another faith-based film.

Meanwhile, my relationship with my daughter stopped being a task. When I was selfish, I struggled with being a mom because I felt like I needed so much. When I took the time to become whole, I found I actually did have something left to give my daughter and what I had to give was more than I ever could've imagined. Not only did I have so much to teach her, but she also had a lot to teach me. One time after I tried correcting her outfit before leaving the house she stated, "Mom, you always try to look so perfect before you go anywhere and you always try to make me look so perfect too when the truth is we don't have to. I don't care if my pockets are hanging out or my bow is crooked. You feel like everything has to be so perfect and I don't want that. It's okay if that's what you want and if that matters to you but it doesn't matter to me. So whatever that perfect thing is I don't want it. I'm just fine with my pockets and whatever else is out of place." My daughter was only ten when she said this and I couldn't have been prouder. Over the years, she has said and taught me some amazing things.

Filming began to wrap and the holidays and my thirtieth birthday were approaching. For the first time, I had no fear or reservations. I was at home watching TV when I decided to go on social media. I went through the usual birthday notifications section and I saw Wolf was one of the people who just had a birthday. I wished him a happy birthday and others and I logged off. Later that day, I got an instant message from Wolf. It was small talks at first, the usual "how have you been" conversations. We began to talk on the phone and he proceeded to tell me all about his walk with God and his life change. I couldn't believe it. Wolf had been in and out of prison for a little over a decade. He was not the same Wolf I saw that day all those years ago. He saw that I wasn't the same person either. We began to talk almost every day. Our friendship grew into a friendship I never experienced with a guy before. He offered to take me out for my birthday for dinner. I was terrified. I had been just fine not having to worry about my feelings, or if somebody was cheating on me or lying to me; I was just really comfortable. I wasn't sure I wanted to date because I felt so safe by myself, and with Jesus of course. But I went and almost had a nervous breakdown afterward because I was that afraid. However, I quickly swallowed that fear because I reminded myself that my trust was in God, not in man, so whether it worked or not, I was still going to be okay. I slowly let my guard down and let Wolf wow me with his life change.

When he had gotten out of prison, he completed his education and even furthered it in a career field making more money than me. He was mentoring others and doing public speaking. Wolf was really the type of person that only God could help and he did! He was so preserved, focused, and driven. I admired his decision of being adamant about not having children until he felt all of his selfishness was driven out of him. Wolf was indeed a new man and I was a new woman. Turning thirty ended up being the start of my new life as my new self.

"Therefore if anyone is in Christ, he is a new creature; the old things passed away; behold new things have come."
2 Corinthians 5:17 NLT

Do Wolf and Stacey end up with a happily ever after or will this too end up in shambles? Will Stacey finally get everything she always wanted? Has Stacey really learned from her mistakes? You want to know, don't you? I don't blame you; I'd like to know too! For now, I guess we'll just have to wait and see. Isn't that how life works? We're all just waiting to see what is in store for the future.

Unfortunately, I can't give Stacey any more advice about her life. I've finally caught up to her. After all, I am she and she is me and we haven't lived enough beyond this moment to truly tell you what's next!

I guess if I were to advise myself of anything I'd say, "Don't be so hard on yourself, for we are all broken vessels hoping to be molded into something beautiful!"

About the Author

Yvonne Gurley, award winner of surviving a whole lot of crap and remaining sane enough to tell you about it. Before becoming an author she has been sharing her thoughts and experiences on her blog site www.thoughtsofthetouched.wordpress.com. Yvonne is a student of life and master of mistakes. She has been a mentor to many women and young girls. When she's not writing she's speaking, encouraging others not to suffer in silence be it mental illness, abuse, or life's hard knocks in general. She lives to inspire and motivate others.

www.ingramcontent.com/pod-product-compliance
Lightning Source LLC
Chambersburg PA
CBHW021056080526
44587CB00010B/269